THE BEST ATTORNEY NEVER WINS

THE BEST ATTORNEY NEVER WINS

WHY GREAT LAWYERS GO BROKE AND AVERAGE ONES BUILD EMPIRES

ANGELO PERONE

THE BEST ATTORNEY NEVER WINS
Why Great Lawyers Go Broke and Average Ones Build Empires

FIRST EDITION

ISBN   978-1-5445-5315-3 *Hardcover*
        978-1-5445-5314-6 *Paperback*
        978-1-5445-5316-0 *Ebook*

CONTENTS

PREFACE..9

INTRODUCTION 15

1. WHY THE BEST ATTORNEY NEVER WINS 23

2. THE RAINMAKER (SALES TO MANY)................................37

3. THE CLOSER (SALES TO ONE) 51

4. THE ARCHITECT (SYSTEMS THAT SCALE) 71

5. THE RIGHT PEOPLE IN THE RIGHT SEATS......................89

6. LAWYER TO CEO (THE ENDGAME) 103

7. THE SHARKS ARE COMING..117

EPILOGUE 129

PREFACE

THE BATTLE YOU'RE LOSING

I WAS SITTING OUT BACK WITH MY LAPTOP, TRYING TO GET some sun. One of those eighty-degree days where everything feels alive. The kind of afternoon where the world is doing its thing and you feel like you're doing yours.

My phone rang. A Louisiana number.

The first time Jim called me, he sounded like a guy who had it figured out. He was a personal injury attorney. Had a decent staff. Had cases coming in. I could hear it through the phone. Another line ringing in the background. Someone's voice down the hall, asking about a filing. The ambient hum of a practice that was breathing. He had a nice little operation that paid the bills and kept the lights on; he'd heard about Case Connect, and he wanted to know what we could do for him.

I walked him through the whole thing. Marketing. Intake. Case acquisition at scale. The system. The math. All of it. He listened. Asked good questions. Took his time. There was no urgency in his voice. He sounded like a man browsing, not shopping. Like someone standing in a showroom with his hands in his pockets, nodding at the cars but in no rush to buy one.

He said: "Let me think about it."

I told him the door was open whenever he was ready.

The second time Jim called me was about a year later. He started the conversation with a joke I don't remember. I remember the laugh that came after it. It arrived a half-second too late, like he'd rehearsed it on the way to dialing my number. He asked the same questions he'd asked the first time, but faster. He'd start a sentence, stop, restart it with different words. At one point he asked me something I'd already answered two minutes earlier. He apologized. Said he had a lot going on.

I found out later he'd let a couple of staff members go. Case volume was down. He was still practicing, still fighting, still grinding. But something underneath had shifted and he could feel it even if he couldn't name it yet.

I walked him through everything again. Same system. Same math. Same opportunity.

He said: "Let me think about it."

The third time, Jim asked to do a Google Meet. I said sure.

When the call connected, I wasn't looking at a man in an office. Jim was sitting outside on the front porch of a place that didn't look like where a fourteen-year veteran of personal injury law should be sitting. He was on his phone, not a computer. The camera was too close to his face. Behind him was a railing, some siding, a quiet street. No office. No conference room. No staff walking past a doorway.

He tried to sound excited. Tried to sound like a guy calling to make a big move. But his eyes kept drifting off-camera, like part of him was somewhere else entirely. He wasn't 100 percent there. He'd ask a question, I'd answer it, and there'd be a pause where he was supposed to respond but didn't. Like the words were reaching him on a delay.

He told me he wanted to start buying cases. He asked about pricing. He asked about volume. He asked all the right questions. But as I sat there looking at this man on a porch that wasn't his office, I realized what had happened.

His staff was gone. All of them. His case volume had dried up. He wasn't calling from a firm anymore. He was alone, sitting outside a place that didn't look like his, calling me because he didn't know what else to do.

And I had to tell him no.

I leaned back in my chair and closed my eyes for a second before I said it. Not because I didn't want to help him. Because I couldn't. He didn't have the infrastructure to work the leads. He didn't have the staff to answer the phones. He didn't have the money to sustain a campaign long enough for it to work. Three years earlier, he could have done this. Two years earlier, he still had a shot. But he waited. He "thought about it" until there was nothing left to think about.

I wasn't going to take this man's last dollar. Not when I knew, in my gut, that he wasn't set up to succeed. That would've made me who I hate most in this industry: someone who takes money from a desperate person and watches them drown.

The silence after I told him sat there for a long time. Jim nodded slowly. He said something like, "I understand." But his eyes were still drifting off-camera, looking at something I couldn't see. Then he thanked me. That was the part that got me. He thanked me.

Jim closed his practice. Last I heard, he took a job at someone else's firm. I never heard from him again. Sometimes I drive past office buildings and wonder if one of them used to be his. If his name used to be on the door. If there's a lobby somewhere with a hole in the wall where his sign used to hang. A good attorney. A smart attorney. An attorney who could have helped a lot of people and built something real. Gone. Because he let fear make every decision for him until fear was the only thing he had left.

That story keeps me up at night.

Because Jim isn't rare. There are over 48,000 personal injury firms in this country. Half of them won't survive five years. And that might be the generous number. My gut tells me 40 percent won't make it through the next decade. Not because the attorneys aren't talented. Because they're playing a game nobody taught them the rules to. Law school taught them how to practice law. It didn't teach them how to find clients. It didn't teach them how to build systems. It didn't teach them how to run a business. And the gap between being a great attorney and running a great firm is where careers go to die.

I'm not an attorney. I'm the guy attorneys call when they're ready to stop losing.

I've spent over $200 million in advertising in the personal injury space. I run a company that does over $50 million a year and is on pace for its biggest year ever. I've helped scale over 120 law firms. I've watched attorneys go from maxed-out credit cards to eight-figure exits. I've watched solo practitioners build machines that print money while they sleep.

And I've watched attorneys like Jim wait until there was nothing left to save.

This book is everything I know. The system. The math. The psychology. The playbook that those eight-figure firms don't want you to have. Every chapter teaches you something real, something specific, something you can use whether you ever work with me or not. But I'm going to be straight with you from the first page: The clock is ticking. There are forces coming into this industry right now that are going to make what happened to Jim look like a warm-up. The window to build your firm into something that can survive what's coming is open right now. It won't be open forever.

You can think about it.

Or you can turn the page.

INTRODUCTION

MY JOURNEY TO THE TRUTH

I WAS PACING AROUND MY DINING ROOM WHEN TYLER CALLED. It was one of those evenings where the whole house had finally gone still. My daughter was asleep upstairs. No TV. No noise. Just the kind of quiet where you can hear yourself think, which is exactly the kind of quiet you don't want when you're about to get the worst phone call of your young career.

Tyler Wilk was a personal injury attorney who'd been fired from his firm for trying to bring in cases on the side. He was sitting on a law degree, a maxed-out credit card, and zero clients. I told him I'd run ads for his firm. I told him I could make it work.

The first ad I ever ran for his firm was called "GOT WILK?" Like the milk campaign. Clever branding. Catchy slogan. I thought I was being creative.

It bombed. Completely.

Tyler hadn't signed a single case. Not one. His voice on the phone wasn't angry. It was worse than that. It was the voice of a guy who trusted someone and was starting to realize that trust might have been misplaced. He didn't know exactly how much we'd spent. I did. Thousands of dollars. Gone. I stopped pacing. I pulled up the Facebook dashboard and stared at the numbers and felt my stomach drop through the floor.

This wasn't a "learning experience." This was a man with no plan B who had bet on me, and I was failing him. Tyler needed this to work. He didn't have a safety net. He didn't have a fall-back firm waiting to take him back. He had a maxed-out credit card and a friend who promised him advertising would change everything. And that friend had just burned through his money making a milk commercial.

I sat with that feeling for a while. The weight of it. The shame of letting someone down who trusted you with every-thing they had. If you've ever been responsible for someone else's outcome and watched it go sideways, you know exactly what I'm talking about. It sits on your chest like a cinder block.

And then something happened. Not a lightbulb. Not some genius revelation. Desperation.

I was in my dining room, leaning back against the stone ledger wall. The jagged edges pressed into my spine through my shirt. Cold and rough, even in the dead of summer. The kind of wall that won't let you get comfortable against it. The house was dark and quiet, nothing but the low hum of the HVAC push-ing against the heat. The Facebook dashboard was still glowing on my laptop across the room, and in the six-foot mirror on the opposite wall I could see my own face lit by nothing but that screen. Tyler's money, gone. My credibility, on the line. And I was staring at my own reflection, those jagged edges digging into my back like the question I couldn't stop asking.

Why the hell am I trying to be like *them*?

Why was I copying firms with millions of dollars in budget who can plaster mediocre, self-serving ads all over the internet with no regard for what they're spending or whether anything actually converts? I couldn't play that game. I didn't have the money to play that game. And I shouldn't have been playing it in the first place. Because I already knew what worked. I'd spent years proving it.

I'd spent a decade in fitness learning how to make people in pain trust me enough to take action. And I was throwing all of that away to copy the people who were already losing.

So I stopped doing what they did. And I started doing what I knew.

Everything I'd learned in a decade of fitness marketing. Sitting across from people in pain. Finding the nerve. Learning what makes a scared person say yes. I compressed it all into one ad. I grabbed one of Tyler's actual settlement checks. Filmed myself holding it. Shot the whole thing from the perspective of a client who'd just gotten paid, as if they were the one telling the story. Shaky camera. Raw audio. Unpolished. It looked like a real person sharing a secret with their friends, not a law firm selling a service. The message was simple: If you've been in a car accident, click this link and we'll review your situation for free.

It didn't just work. It detonated.

The cost per lead came back at a third of what I'd been paying on the GOT WILK? campaign. A third. Tyler signed his first case within forty-eight hours of the leads going live. Then another. Then another. He went from zero cases to over 200 in his first year. He was a millionaire by year two. To his credit, once he saw it working, he didn't get cautious. He tripled down. He reinvested everything back into the machine and kept feeding it.

I remember early on, when the results first started hitting, Tyler looked at me and said: "We have to make a business out of this." I said: "You're my first client. This is already a business."

But the road between "this is already a business" and what Case Connect became had a crater in the middle.

Before Tyler, I'd failed more than once. A tattoo parlor. A concrete company. Businesses that blew up in my face before I understood what I was doing wrong. When the concrete company collapsed, my father put his hand on my shoulder and told me it was okay. He meant it as love. But standing there, hearing my father give me permission to fail, something turned in my stomach. Because "it's okay" sounded a lot like "this is who you are." Like mediocrity was something I should learn to live with. And every single thing I've built since that moment has been my answer to that sentence.

But the failure that finally taught me something useful was a gym franchise that became the number one in the country in its first year. I was on the highway, Apple CarPlay connected, when Coach Tim called me. Tim was the manager I'd hired to run the floor. Salt of the earth guy. The kind of person who shows up early, stays late, and treats every member like family. He told me they'd just crushed a record challenge. Converted more members than any month I'd been on the floor. And for the first time, I hadn't been in the building. I hadn't trained a single one of them. I hadn't touched anything.

I screamed "Let's gooooo!" so loud it probably rattled the speakers. Not just because the numbers were good. Because Tim did it. A man I believed in, running a system I built, producing results better than I could have produced myself. That's the lesson underneath every chapter in this book. The system is the product. Not you.

That lesson was sitting right there in my head when Tyler's results exploded. I needed to know if it would work for someone who wasn't my best friend. Someone I'd never met. A real client. A real test.

His name was Joey. California attorney. Small firm. Making a few hundred grand a year. I pitched him on a Zoom call from my kitchen island, sitting on a stool with a MacBook Pro and my daughter Aria asleep on my chest. It was the middle of the afternoon. My wife was passed out upstairs because none of us slept at night with the baby. That kitchen island was Case Connect's headquarters. A stool, a laptop, and a sleeping newborn. That's what a $50 million company looked like on day one.

Joey was the easiest pitch I've ever made. Cool. Down to earth. Easy to talk to. The call went smoother than I expected. But when I hung up, the nerves hit. It worked for Tyler. But Tyler was my boy. This was a different state. A different firm. A different human being. If it didn't work for Joey, maybe Tyler was just a fluke.

Joey's first month, we spent about $1,600 on ads. He signed 7 or 8 cases.

He called me. "How much did we spend?"

"About sixteen hundred."

"No fucking way. You gotta be kidding me. Is this a scam?"

It wasn't a scam. It was the same system doing what it was designed to do. Joey kept going. He kept investing. He kept tripling down the way Tyler did. He hired intake staff. Trained them. Treated every client like family. Within two years, Joey sold his firm for mid-eight-figures. Two years. From a few hundred grand to a life-changing exit.

He called me after the sale. Not to talk business. To tell me how much he appreciated me and what I meant to his success. I call him my brother. He trusted me, he held up his end of the bargain, and he built something most attorneys will never come close to. And he's not done. He's going for rounds two and three right now.

One afternoon, a brand-new Rolls Royce Spectre pulled

into my driveway. Mandarin interior. Tyler behind the wheel, grinning like a kid on Christmas. A few years earlier, neither of us had shit. I put my daughters in the back seat, and they ran their little fingers across the leather, stared up at the roof full of fiber-optic lights, and called it the "star car." Tyler stood in the driveway watching them, and neither of us said anything for a second. We didn't need to. The car said it.

Case Connect grew from $12 million in year one to over $50 million annually. We're on pace for the biggest year in the company's history. Just recently, I was at a restaurant in Margate with my wife and our three girls. All three of them under six. My oldest was coloring on the placemat. My youngest was trying to eat a crayon. A normal Tuesday. Then an attorney at another table grabbed my arm, stood up, and started telling the entire restaurant I was famous. That he followed everything I did. My wife was cracking up. She had no idea. At home, I'm not a CEO. I'm not the guy who's spent $200 million on ads. I'm Daddy. I'm the one who puts them to bed and gets asked to play tea party. And here was a grown man in a restaurant telling strangers about me while my daughter tried to eat a Crayola.

I'm not showing off. I'm showing you what's possible when the system works and you're willing to bet on yourself. Because somewhere out there, right now, is an attorney who feels the way I felt standing in that dark dining room, staring at my own reflection. Like the successful people are operating on a different level. Like there's some secret they know that you don't. Like you're stuck on the outside looking in.

There is no secret. There's a system. The same system that took Tyler from a maxed-out credit card to a Rolls-Royce in my driveway. The same system that took Joey from a few hundred grand to an eight-figure exit. The same system that turned a shaky video of a settlement check into a machine that generates over $50 million a year. I'm going to hand it to you, piece by piece, chapter by chapter, in this book.

One more thing before we go any further. I own a company that does everything I'm about to teach you. You'll figure that out in about three chapters. I'm not hiding it. But every chapter in this book gives you the real playbook. The whole thing. Not a teaser. Not a sample with a pitch at the end. The actual system. If you take what I teach you and build a machine that eats my lunch, I'll shake your hand and mean it. Some of you will read this book and call me. Some of you will read it and do it yourselves. Either way, you'll have everything you need. That's not a sales pitch. That's a promise.

But there's something I need you to understand before we start. Half the firms in this industry won't exist in five years. And the thing that's killing them isn't a bad economy, or ambulance chasers, or too many attorneys. It's something most of them do every single day without realizing it's destroying them.

CHAPTER 1

WHY THE BEST ATTORNEY NEVER WINS

I WAS STANDING AT MY KITCHEN ISLAND THE OTHER NIGHT. Kids were finally asleep. The house was quiet. That 8:30 p.m. window where the chaos stops and I can actually hear my own brain.

The counter was still covered in papers from my daughter's schoolbag. Permission slips. A worksheet with her name written in crayon. A drawing of Elsa from *Frozen* with purple hair because she ran out of yellow. I hadn't looked at any of them. They'd been sitting there all week, waiting for a version of me that wasn't buried in dashboards and Slack threads. Little paper witnesses to the fact that I'd been choosing the business over the backpack every single night.

I wasn't looking for anything. Just scrolling Instagram the way everyone does when their brain needs to shut off for five minutes. Then I stopped. I went back and started counting.

Nine posts in my feed. Four of them were ads for personal injury attorneys.

I screen-recorded it and sent it to my business partner. "Look at this. This is insane." He texted back something like "that's crazy" and moved on. I don't think he understood what I was looking at. Not the ads themselves. The velocity. The sheer volume of competition flooding a space that most attorneys still think runs on referrals and reputation.

But here's the part that really messed with me. Every single one of those ads was a knockoff. Stolen hooks. Stolen angles. Recycled concepts that I recognized because I created the originals. Temu versions of ads my team built that actually worked, now being copied by people who have no idea *why* they worked, running them into the ground until they don't work for anyone anymore. Bits and pieces of my playbook Frankenstein'd together and thrown against the wall by people who couldn't tell you the first thing about what makes a human being in pain pick up their phone and ask for help.

Four out of nine. And that's just what I saw in five minutes on a Tuesday night.

If you're a PI attorney and you're not running aggressive, targeted advertising right now, that's what's happening behind your back. Every person in your city who gets into an accident is getting targeted by dozens of hungry attorneys and marketing companies before they leave the hospital parking lot. This is a different world. A different game. The old players need to evolve or retire. There is no third option.

All of that is happening behind your back while you sit there waiting for the phone to ring.

THE PHONE THAT STOPPED RINGING

I was sitting in my office a few months ago when this call came in. A guy named Dave. He'd responded to one of our email campaigns about case acquisition. Twenty-two years in practice. Built his firm the old-fashioned way. SEO. Referrals. Reputation.

Dave had a slow crawl to his voice. The kind of voice that sounds like it's never been in a rush for anything. Like every word has to pass through a tollbooth before it reaches his mouth. Under normal circumstances, it probably made clients feel safe. Like they were in steady hands.

For two decades, it worked. People walked through the door. The phone rang. Cases showed up like clockwork. He never had to think about where the next client was coming from because the next client always came.

Then one year, the phone rang a little less. He didn't panic. Slow months happen. The next year, it rang even less. He told himself the market was soft. By the time he called me, that slow crawl in his voice had something else underneath it. A tightness I've heard hundreds of times. The voice of a man who's been telling everyone things are fine while quietly watching his life's work evaporate.

"The phones just don't ring anymore," he said. "I don't know what happened. We used to have people walking in off the street. Now nothing."

I asked him what he was doing to generate cases. He told me about his SEO. His referral network. His reputation in the community. All the things that worked for twenty years.

I said: "And how's that going?"

Silence. The crawl in his voice finally stopped. Because there was nothing left to say slowly.

I sat listening to that silence, and I just felt bad for the guy. I knew exactly what was happening to him. The referral network that fed him for twenty years dried up. His SEO got buried by firms spending $30,000 a month on ads to sit above his organic listing. The reputation he spent a career building became invisible because nobody searches for "best attorney in town" anymore. They click the first ad that speaks to their pain.

And here's the part that sat with me long after I hung up. Even if I could fix his marketing tomorrow, even if I could flood his phone with leads by next week, he wasn't equipped to convert any of them. His intake process was built for a world where clients walked through the door already sold. Warm referrals. People who showed up ready to sign. He'd never had to sell anyone on anything in his life because the clients came pre-sold.

That world is gone. And it's never coming back.

What kept me up that night wasn't this one attorney. It was the math. There are 48,000 personal injury firms in this country. Half of them won't survive five years.

And most of them are good people. Great attorneys. People who went to law school to help the injured. They're going to get eaten alive. Not because they're bad at their jobs. Because the game changed underneath them, and nobody told them the rules.

THE ONE QUESTION NOBODY CAN ANSWER

I got on a Zoom a while back with an attorney who had offices in Texas and Alabama. This man came in *hot*. Leaned back in his chair. Chest puffed. The confidence was dripping off the screen.

He had his whole team lined up on the call like he was presenting his cabinet to Congress. A CMO. A social media manager. A "marketing expert." And some other title I can't even remember. Four people. All dedicated to marketing for a single law firm.

The attorney went first. Told me how incredible his team was. Best in the business. Nobody does it like they do. The CMO sat there nodding like a bobblehead. The social media manager looked proud. The marketing expert smiled.

They were eating it up. Their boss was praising them in front of a stranger, and they were basking in it like cats in a sunbeam.

I looked at that screen with four faces on it and did the math in my head. These people were costing this firm somewhere between $300,000 and $400,000 a year in salary alone. Before ad spend. Before tools. Before overhead. Four hundred grand a year in payroll for people whose entire job was to bring in cases.

So I asked the question. The same question I ask on every call. The one question that tells me everything I need to know about a firm in under ten seconds.

"What's your cost per case?"

The room shifted. The CMO's nod stopped mid-bob. The social media manager looked down. The marketing expert started talking about impressions and engagement rates. Nobody answered the question. Because nobody knew.

Four hundred thousand dollars a year. And not one of them could tell me the single most important number in their entire operation.

Then the attorney chimed in. "We convert 95 percent of our leads."

I said what I always say when I hear that number: "If that's true, I'm shutting down my company tomorrow and coming to work for you."

He laughed. I wasn't laughing.

Nobody converts 95 percent. Not us. Not anyone. But firms believe it because they've never actually measured it. Their team tells them the number, and they swallow it whole.

And here's what makes it even more insane: If you're converting 95 percent of your leads, why are you on a Zoom with me shopping for a marketing company? If your team is the best in the business, why is the phone not ringing? Something doesn't add up. But nobody in that room was asking the question because doing so would mean admitting that the $400,000-a-year marketing team wasn't what the boss said it was.

Here's what happened next. He started buying leads from us. Same firm. Same market. Same four-person team. And they couldn't make a single outside source work. Not ours. Not anyone's.

Every vendor they'd ever tried had "bad leads." Every source was "garbage." Every marketing company was "a scam." The team's story never changed. Their process was perfect. They just needed to find the "right marketing." Meanwhile, the marketing was sitting in their inbox dying because their flawless team wouldn't pick up the phone and call it.

These firms are profitable. Some of them very profitable. But here's the part that should terrify you: They're profitable by accident.

I learned this from selling cars. I'd watch customers walk onto that showroom floor already sold. They'd done the research. Picked the model. Driven forty minutes to the dealership. And they'd end up buying from the worst rep on the floor. Not because of him. Despite him. He'd fumble the pitch, forget the financing options, couldn't explain a single feature under the hood. Didn't matter. The customer wanted the car so badly that they would buy it from a mannequin.

That's how most PI firms operate. Clients show up pre-sold through referrals or reputation, and the firm closes them, calling it a system. It's not a system. It's a streak. And streaks end. When you can't measure what's actually working, you can't fix it when it stops. And when you can't fix it, someone who *can* will come into your market and take every case you thought was yours.

There's a part of Joey's story I didn't tell you in the Introduction. The part that matters most.

About six to nine months after he started running ads, something happened that he didn't expect. His phone started ringing with calls that didn't come from us. People he'd signed months earlier were sending him everyone they knew.

"I had a passenger in the car. Can you handle their case too?" One case became two. Sometimes three. "My mom was in an accident last week. Can she call you?" "My brother got rear-ended. I told him you're the only person to call."

The referrals showed up on top of the paid marketing. Joey didn't spend an extra dollar to get them. They came because he'd done the work. He acquired clients through marketing. Converted them through intake. Treated them like family. Built systems so nothing fell through the cracks. And the machine started feeding itself.

That's the flywheel. Marketing brings clients in. Intake converts them. Systems keep them. And the clients themselves become the engine that multiplies everything without costing you an extra dollar. Reviews. Referrals. Repeat cases. The flywheel spins faster with every rotation. It's the reason Joey went from a few hundred grand to a mid-eight-figure exit in two years. Not because he was the best attorney in California. Because he built the machine and fed it until it took on a life of its own.

Most attorneys never get there because they never get past step one. They're still waiting for the phone to ring the way it rang ten years ago. Or they tried marketing once, got burned by some hack who stole my ad templates and charged them $15,000 for a course, and decided the whole thing was a scam.

It's not a scam. You just hired the wrong people. And while

you were swearing off marketing, the attorneys who figured this out pulled away so fast it looks unfair from the outside.

SIGNING THE CLIENT IS JUST THE BEGINNING

I need to tell you something that most attorneys don't want to hear.

When you sign a client, you haven't won anything. The game has just begun.

We signed a case in Texas. A daughter had passed away. The mother was the one who called us. Catastrophic case. Potentially seven figures.

Our team did everything right. Connected with the mother. Built trust. Handled every detail with care. She signed. We handed the case to the firm.

Two weeks later, I saw a credit request come through. The firm wanted their money back for the case.

I got on a call and asked what happened. They told me the mother had gone with another attorney. I asked how many times they'd spoken with her after the handoff. Twice. They talked to this woman twice in two weeks, and then she stopped answering. By the time they reached her, she was already represented by someone else.

And they wanted us to credit the case. Like it was our fault.

Think about what happened here. A mother who just lost her daughter called us in the worst moment of her life. Our team connected with her. Made her feel heard. Made her feel safe. Signed her up.

And then she got handed off to a firm that called her twice in two weeks during the most painful experience a human being can go through.

Meanwhile, every other firm in the state was calling her.

Texting her. Running ads in front of her. Someone showed up who made her feel more cared for than the firm that was supposed to be fighting for her. And she left.

It's like marrying the most beautiful woman in the world and then ignoring her. Then sending her out to a bar full of GQ models driving Ferraris. What exactly do you think is going to happen?

Once you sign someone, every firm in the country is still calling them. Their uncle Bob is telling them he knows a guy who'll do it cheaper. Insurance adjusters are in their ear. The second you go quiet, you're done. They will sub out and sign with the next person who makes them feel like they matter. And you'll be left staring at a credit request, wondering what went wrong.

I'll show you later in this book exactly how to build a wall around your clients so this never happens. For now, just understand this: Signing the case isn't the finish line. It's the starting gun.

THE CASE EVERYONE CALLED A LOSER

Here's where I need to rewire how you think about money.

The nationwide average fee to a firm on cases like ours, not counting the monster settlements, is $18,000. If you're acquiring cases for $2,000 to $4,000, the front-end math already works before you factor in anything else.

But the front-end math isn't even the real play.

I have a firm in Florida. They took a case from us. Parking lot accident. Low property damage. Minor injuries. The at-fault party had a $10,000 policy in a state where that's the minimum. There wasn't much to work with.

On paper, this was a loser. The firm probably lost money on

it. Most attorneys would look at that and say: "See? Marketing doesn't work." Case closed. Back to praying for referrals.

The attorney called me a while later. He was telling me about this client. She'd been a handful. Demanding. Called a lot. But his team decided to treat her right anyway. Do the right thing. Help her even though the case wasn't going to pay the bills.

Then he told me what happened next.

That woman referred five other cases to his firm over the next two years. She told everyone. Her family. Her friends. Her coworkers. Anyone who got into any kind of accident heard about this attorney because this one woman wouldn't shut up about how well they treated her.

One of those five referrals was a multiple-surgery commercial vehicle case. The kind of case that changes a firm's entire year.

The attorney was laughing when he told me. He called her a "referral machine." A parking lot fender bender with a $10,000 policy turned into a pipeline of high-value cases because one attorney decided to treat a "loser" client like she mattered.

Nobody in this space thinks about clients as equity. Everyone evaluates marketing on a case-by-case snapshot. They pay $3,000 for a case. It settles for less than expected. "Bad ROI." Stop spending. That thinking will keep you small forever.

Every client you acquire becomes equity in your firm. They get into another accident in two years. Who do they call? You. Their cousin gets rear-ended. Who do they refer? You. They leave a five-star review at midnight that a stranger reads while deciding who to call. Who does that stranger call? You.

The big cases don't come from ads. The people with major injuries, the ones looking at six- and seven-figure settlements, they *know* they have a case. They come through referrals. From people you already helped who trust you enough to send their family your way. You build that network by acquiring volume. You acquire volume by investing in marketing. And the whole thing starts by understanding that every client is an asset, not an expense.

When you get this, everything changes. When you don't, you'll always find a reason to stop spending.

WHAT'S COMING FOR YOU

I've shown you the lie. I've shown you the math. I've shown you what happens when the machine is built right, and I've shown you what happens when it's not.

Now I need to tell you something that should scare you more than anything else in this book.

A few months ago, I walked into a call center. Not mine. One run by a group of operators from solar, ACA, and Medicare. Industries where you have to convince a healthy person to spend money they don't want to spend on a product they're not sure they need. That's an NBA-level game. Personal injury, where you're telling an injured person you'll get them money for free? To these people, that's JV.

The energy in that room hit me like a wall. Two hundred seats filled. Phones ringing on top of phones ringing. These people weren't making calls. They were hunting.

I talked to one of the guys running the floor. He'd sold companies, taken them public, bought them back, done it all over again. I asked him why he was looking at personal injury.

He didn't even hesitate. "You're selling free money. The client is already hurt. They already need a lawyer. And the attorneys in this space?" He shook his head. "Lazy. Inefficient. They have no idea what's about to hit them."

They're already buying up firms. Already deploying tech

stacks that cost more per month than most PI firms make in a year. It already happened in solar. It already happened in Medicare. The same playbook is being run on personal injury right now. Later in this book, I'll tell you exactly what they're doing and how to survive it. But the window to prepare is closing faster than you think.

WHAT IT LOOKS LIKE WHEN IT WORKS

I'd just finished a late lunch at my desk. Half a sandwich was still sitting next to my keyboard, wrapper peeled back, close enough that I kept nudging it out of frame every time I reached for something. The kind of meal you eat standing up between calls because sitting down for it would mean admitting you have time you don't actually have. Tyler was in one corner of my screen, John in another, and Ryan's tile was buffering. Choppy video. Frozen frames. I figured he was calling from his car between depositions, fighting cell service on some Midwest highway.

Then his camera caught up to his voice and the frame sharpened, and I wasn't looking at a highway.

I was looking at a cabin that belonged in a magazine nobody sends me. Cream leather so clean it looked like it had never been touched. Dark stitching running along every edge like someone had sewn the whole thing by hand. The ceiling was high enough that nobody ducked. The seats faced each other. The light inside was soft, even, the kind of light that doesn't come from a window. It came from the plane itself, like the air had been designed along with everything else.

Ryan was talking about his cases the way a man talks about lawn care. Easy. Handled. Nothing urgent. He flipped the camera across the aisle. His buddy was sitting in a matching leather seat, head down, scrolling his phone the way people scroll when a private jet is just where they happen to be on a Tuesday. He looked up. Threw a hand. Half a nod. Half a smile. Then right back to scrolling. The whole exchange lasted two seconds. It said everything.

They were flying from Formula One in Miami to Vail. Skiing. Then back to the Midwest, where Ryan's firm would be running the same way it ran when he left. The same way it ran every day. His intake was built. His systems were documented. His team didn't call him when he was gone because there was nothing to call about. The machine just hummed.

I watched his face. No tightness behind his eyes. No phone buzzing with fires he had to put out. That weightless look you only see in a person who built something that works without their hands on it every second of every day. The opposite of every managing partner I've ever watched grind through midnight with knots in their shoulders and dread sitting on their chest like a cinder block.

Something settled in me. Not envy. I've never once felt envious watching someone win. It's always the same thing. A pull. A compass needle swinging hard toward a point on the horizon I haven't reached yet. I looked at Ryan's face on that screen, the cabin behind him bright and still and quiet, and I thought: That's it. That's what I'm helping build. Not cases. Not revenue. That. The relief. The freedom. The feeling of a man who built a machine that runs without him and now gets to live inside the life he earned instead of staring at it through a screen.

Every attorney works for that feeling whether they know it or not. Most will never get there. Not because they can't. Because they won't do the things this book is about to teach them.

But first, I need to show you what's coming for the ones who don't.

WHAT'S NEXT

A firm spent $100,000 on marketing in a single month and signed 5 cases. Then I changed one thing. Just one. Same ads. Same budget. Same leads. Fifty-seven signed cases the next month. Over 1,000 percent improvement.

I'll tell you what that one thing was. But not yet.

The answer starts in the back office of a gym, with a woman who didn't come to talk about a membership.

CHAPTER 2

THE RAINMAKER (SALES TO MANY)

THE BACK OFFICE OF A GYM IS NOT WHERE ANYONE GOES TO fall apart. It's a cramped room with fluorescent lights, worn chairs that wobble when you shift your weight, and a small window that doesn't look outside. It looks into the gym floor. With the door closed, you can't hear the music from the classes. You can feel it. A low bass drone that hums in your chest like a second heartbeat.

I was sitting across from a woman I'll call Sandy. She'd come in to talk about a membership. That's what she said. But nobody walks into a gym and sits down in a back office just to talk about equipment and class schedules.

I started asking questions. Not about fitness. About her. And the surface cracked fast.

Sandy had lost both her parents. Not to an accident. To neglect. They didn't take care of themselves, and she carried that with her every day. The grief of watching people she loved choose not to fight for their own lives. The resentment she couldn't shake. She'd just come from her doctor. The news wasn't good. Insulin. Metformin. The same road her parents walked.

And then she looked at her kids. She told me she looked at her children and felt the exact pain that had hollowed her out for years, except now she was the one doing it to them. She was becoming the thing she'd spent her whole life being angry about. Sitting in a wobbling chair in the back of a gym, under fluorescent lights, with bass thumping through the walls, she broke.

I didn't sell her a gym membership. I showed her how we were going to make sure her kids never sat where she was sitting. We were going to get her eating right. Training. Building something her body could sustain. Not because she wanted to look a certain way. Because she wanted to live.

She signed. Not because of a discount or a promotion. Because I found the nerve.

That's the skill nobody teaches in any marketing course. Not how to run a Facebook ad. Not how to optimize a landing page. How to sit across from a human being in real pain and connect with the thing that's actually driving them. The surface reason is never the real reason. The real reason is underneath, and it's almost always about someone they love.

Every potential client you'll ever reach is tuned into one station. WIIFM. What's In It For Me. Not your awards. Not your track record. Not your law school credentials. Can you solve *my* problem, and why should I trust *you*? That's it. If you're not broadcasting to that station, nothing you say will ever reach them.

I spent a decade learning how to broadcast to that station in one of the most ruthless marketing environments on earth: fitness. Hand-to-hand combat. Every single day. Gyms on every corner running the same ads. Razor-thin margins. In that world, you learn fast or you die. You learn how to find the nerve and show someone a path forward they actually believe in. And I was good at it. Better than anyone I competed against.

So when I looked at the personal injury space for the first time, I couldn't believe what I was seeing.

Every ad was the same. Attorney in a suit. Arms crossed. Standing in front of a bookshelf or a courthouse. "Injured? Call us. We fight for you. Over $100 million recovered."

I sat there staring at my screen, thinking: *These people have no idea what they're doing.*

They were broadcasting about themselves. Their awards. Their results. Their experience. Not a single ad spoke to the person sitting on their couch with a neck brace, a stack of medical bills, and a pit in their stomach, wondering how they were going to pay rent this month. Not one. It was as if the entire industry had agreed to do marketing the worst possible way and nobody had bothered to question it.

I saw a gap so wide you could drive a truck through it.

So here's what I did. I took everything I learned in fitness. The emotional selling. The pain-first approach. The ability to meet someone exactly where they are and speak their language instead of talking over their head. And I built ads that broke every rule personal injury marketing had ever followed.

My ads didn't look like ads. They looked like a real person sharing a secret with their friends. Like someone who'd been in an accident, discovered something they didn't know existed, and was telling everyone about it. The tone wasn't "we're the best law firm." The tone was "holy crap, did you know you can actually do this?"

I threw stones at the institutions my audience was already skeptical of. Insurance companies that lowball injured people.

The confusing legal system that makes victims feel powerless. The idea that hiring an attorney is complicated or expensive. I positioned myself as the antithesis of everything they'd been taught to distrust.

I didn't educate. I didn't overqualify. I didn't dump legal jargon on people. I spoke at a fifth-grade level because that's what connects. I made it simple. I made it feel safe. And I made it feel like *their* idea, not mine.

Then a lead came in. A rear-end collision. Someone who needed help.

Then a surgery case.

Then a motorcycle accident. A guy was riding his bike when an eighteen-wheeler hit him and dragged him two blocks down the road. Two blocks. He was in a coma. His mother was sitting at home, terrified, scrolling her phone at three in the morning, looking for answers, and she saw one of our ads. It resonated with her. She opted in. That case became one of our first monster cases. The kind of case attorneys dream about.

And that's when I realized something. The ads weren't just generating leads. They were reaching people at the most vulnerable, desperate, emotional moments of their lives. Because the ads spoke *to them*. Not at them. Not over them. To them. The way a friend would. The way someone who actually understood their pain would. That's why the mother of a man in a coma, at three in the morning, with tears in her eyes, clicked on our ad instead of scrolling past the hundred attorney billboards she'd already ignored.

The leads kept coming. The cost per lead was a fraction of what the industry considered normal. The conversion rates were absurd. I remember sitting at my desk watching the dashboard tick up and thinking: *This can't be right. Something must be broken. Nobody gets results like this.*

Nothing was broken. It was working exactly the way it was supposed to. Because when you actually understand how to connect with a human being in pain, and you put that understanding into an ad that reaches thousands of people, it's like finding an infinite money glitch. You spend a dollar, and ten dollars come back. You spend a hundred, and a thousand comes back. And it just keeps going.

I didn't just enter the personal injury marketing space. I detonated a bomb in the middle of it.

Within months, every major player in the space was watching what I was doing. Within a year, they were copying it. My landing pages got stolen. My hooks got stolen. My ad angles got stolen. I'm not talking about people being "inspired" by my work. I'm talking about people literally screenshotting my ads, changing the logo, and running them as their own. I've seen my own ads, with Case Connect's name still on them, being run on other people's pages to sell leads to attorneys.

Some of the biggest names in the PI marketing industry were built on the back of my creative work. They copied my formula, slapped their logo on it, and pretended they invented it. To this day, some of the largest PI marketing companies in the country run versions of ads I created years ago.

I should be flattered. I'm not.

But here's what they can never copy: the instinct. The foundational understanding of *why* it works. They can screenshot an ad. They can't screenshot the years I spent sitting across from people in pain, learning how to connect, learning how to listen, learning what makes a human being trust you enough to take action. That's not a template. That's a skill. And by the time they finish copying what I did last year, I've already reinvented the approach. In a year or two, everyone will be copying what I'm doing right now. And I'll have moved on to the next thing.

You're either innovating or imitating. And imitators always eat the dust of the person in front.

THE TWO TRAPS THAT KILL YOUR MARKETING

Most attorneys fall into one of two traps with their advertising. I've watched both traps destroy firms that should have thrived.

I worked with an attorney in Pennsylvania a while back. Smart guy. Ambitious. Had a good firm and wanted to make it bigger. I ran his ads. I showed him the approach, explained the psychology behind it, walked him through why certain angles worked. He watched, he learned, and the numbers were good with us.

Then he decided he could do it himself.

He started running his own ads internally. The stuff he produced couldn't come close to the numbers he got with Case Connect. Not even in the same zip code. So I'd screenshot his ads, rewrite them, and text them back to him with notes explaining why his versions weren't hitting. I literally did his homework for him. For free. Because I wanted him to understand the difference between copying the surface and grasping the foundation.

He eventually branched out on his own. He's doing well now. Plastered on commercials, billboards, acquiring firms in states all over the country. I drove past one of his billboards a while back. My playbook. My angles. My hooks. His name in letters ten feet tall. I sat at that red light staring up at it and felt something I didn't expect. Not anger. Something quieter than that. People talk about him now. They talk about how smart his marketing is. And not one of them knows where it came from. That's the part that sits with you. Not the copying. The credit landing on the wrong doorstep.

I'm not bitter about it. I'm using it to make a point. The

attorney who copies the look of an ad without understanding *why* it works is running what I call the Ego Ad or the Template Ad. And both are killing your marketing.

Trap One: The Ego Ad. This is the attorney who runs ads about themselves. Their results. Their awards. Their experience. "Over $500 million recovered." "Thirty-five years of experience." "Award-winning trial attorneys."

Nobody cares.

I know that stings. You worked your ass off for those results. But your potential client isn't at home applauding your achievements. They're in pain. They're scared. They're overwhelmed. They're wondering how they're going to pay their medical bills and get their car fixed. They're not looking for the most decorated attorney. They're looking for the person who understands what they're going through and can show them the fastest, simplest path to making it better.

Broadcast to WIIFM or fall on deaf ears. Every single time.

Trap Two: The Template Ad. This is the attorney who hired some agency or bought some course and is running cookie-cutter ads that look exactly like every other attorney ad online. Same hooks. Same landing pages. Same promises. Zero differentiation.

And this brings me to something that makes my blood boil.

There are people right now, today, running courses that teach "marketers" how to sell to attorneys. They charge $10 thousand to $15 thousand. They hand over stolen ad templates and a knockoff landing page. And they send these people out into the world to pitch law firms. The person who took the course has zero foundational understanding of why anything works. They just copy and paste. They spin up ads that are a cheap Temu imitation of what actual professionals built, and they sell the leads to any attorney willing to write a check.

What happens next is predictable. The leads are garbage because the person running the ads doesn't understand targeting, messaging, or optimization. The attorney gets frustrated. And here's the part that really burns me: The course teaches these people how to shift the blame. "Your intake is too slow." "Your staff isn't calling fast enough." "Your process is broken." Which might be partially true, but when you can't deliver a quality lead in the first place, blaming the attorney for not converting trash is criminal.

I know of one operation signing up five to ten people *per week* for this kind of program. That's 250 to 500 attorneys per year getting burned by a single outfit. Multiply that across all the copycats in the space, and you start to understand why so many attorneys think marketing "doesn't work."

The damage is real. Every attorney I talk to now is skeptical before the call even starts. They want ninety references. They want case studies and guarantees and proof stacked on top of proof. And I don't blame them. They've been lied to by so many people who ran thousands of dollars in ads, delivered one case, took zero accountability, and disappeared. Nobody in this space is willing to put their money where their mouth is. So when an attorney gets burned, they don't just lose the money. They lose trust in the entire concept. They swear off marketing forever. And while they're swearing it off, the firms that found someone who actually knows what they're doing are pulling away so fast it's not even a fair fight anymore.

Marketing works. You just got scammed by someone who had no business selling it. That's like swearing off restaurants because you got food poisoning at a gas station.

THE CHANNELS THAT ACTUALLY PRINT CASES

Let me tell you what's working right now. Not theory. Not "best practices" from some conference panel. Real data from over $200 million in legal advertising spend.

PPC is our strongest channel, and it's not close. Someone types "car accident lawyer near me," and they're raising their hand saying, "I need help right now." You're not interrupting their day. You're answering their question. Meta still works, but the landscape is a bloodbath. YouTube and Demand Gen let you target based on what people have actually searched, almost like PPC, but deliver video. Programmatic runs ads that look like news articles across blog networks. People engage because the ad looks like it belongs on the page. They think they're reading an article. They're reading your ad. Every one of these channels requires a level of talent and infrastructure that no single firm can replicate. We went through person after person trying to find someone who could run PPC at the level we needed before we found our guy. A data geek who built hundreds of landing pages, split-tested fonts, colors, button positions. Treated every campaign like a science experiment with a six-figure budget. And here's the problem for you: If someone is that good at this, they're never going to work for your firm. They'll spin up their own company and make 100x what you'd pay them. The economics don't work.

But the channel that shocked me most is something most attorneys would never consider in a million years.

My business partner was scrolling one night and saw someone doing QVC-style live streams for a completely different industry. He called me. "You have to see this. This is insane." I watched for thirty seconds and said: "We're doing that tomorrow."

Now picture this: twenty to thirty people going live all day, every day, non-stop. On camera answering questions, engaging with viewers, pointing them to an offer to check if their accident qualifies for compensation. Live television for legal services running twelve hours a day. One of our first streams pulled more qualified leads in a single afternoon than most firms get from a month of Facebook ads. The production required is massive. Most firms couldn't pull it off if they tried. But when it works, it prints cases.

An attorney asked me once which of these channels he should focus on. I told him the truth: all of them. And then I told him the harder truth: You can't. Not by yourself. You went to law school to practice law, not to become an expert in PPC bidding strategies, TikTok live streams, and programmatic ad placement. We do nothing but this. Every single day. We can afford the teams, the technology, and the infrastructure because we have the scale that a single firm never will.

THE ONLY NUMBER THAT MATTERS

I was on a call with an attorney a few months back. Good guy. Smart. Proud of his operation. He told me he was paying his marketing director $180,000 a year. I said: "How many cases has that person generated in the last six months?"

The air left the call. You could feel it through the screen. The attorney's mouth opened, then closed. His eyes shifted to something off-camera, like the answer might be written on the wall behind his monitor. Then his shoulders dropped about half an inch. The kind of drop that happens when a question you've been avoiding finally catches up with you.

"I'd have to check on that and get back to you."

He never did. I already knew the answer. If the number was good, he would have known it the way he knows his own birthday. No hesitation. No checking. The people who are winning always know their numbers. The people who are losing always have to "check."

That call is every call. Attorneys come to me telling me their cost per lead is too high. "Angelo, we're paying $400 a lead. That can't be right."

I always ask the same follow-up. "How many of those leads are you signing?"

"About one in five."

"So your cost per signed case is $2,000. What's the average fee on those cases?"

"Eighteen thousand dollars."

"So you're spending $2,000 to make $18,000 and you're upset about the cost per lead?"

Silence. Every time.

Cost per lead is a vanity metric. It tells you nothing. I don't care about it and neither should you. You can get leads for $50 a piece and sign almost none of them. You can get leads for $500 a piece and sign half of them. The $500 leads might be the better investment by a mile. Firms that chase cheap leads end up drowning their intake team in garbage, burning out their staff, and wondering why their case count isn't growing.

Cost per signed case. That's the only number that matters. And it varies by market. In California, anything with a three in front of it is great. I have firms that are thrilled to pay $4,000 per case, and they wire us millions per month to keep it coming. In Texas, $3,000 to $3,500 is the sweet spot. States like Illinois, Missouri, Pennsylvania, and New Jersey, firms target the $2,000 to $2,500 range.

The average fee to a firm on our cases, excluding the outlier settlements, is $18,000. If you're acquiring cases for $2,000 to $4,000, you don't need a calculator. And that's just the front end. That client becomes equity. Reviews. Referrals. Future cases. The compounding value makes the acquisition cost look like pocket change.

THE MARKETER YOU CAN'T AFFORD TO HIRE

Here's the truth about marketing talent that nobody wants to admit.

If someone is truly great at marketing, they will never work for your firm.

A talented marketer who's actually good at this can get five clients on a pay-per-lead model and clear $25,000 a month working half the hours they'd put in at your firm. They can spin up their own company and make $300 thousand to $500 thousand a year without answering to anyone. Why would they take a salaried position for $150 thousand when they can triple that on their own?

They wouldn't. And they don't.

So firms hire the people who couldn't make it on their own. The person who thinks marketing is posting content on Instagram and measuring success by impressions and likes. Some firm out there right now has a CMO making $300 thousand who doesn't know the first thing about actual client acquisition. They talk about "building the brand." Cool. Show me the money. Cost per case. That's the only conversation worth having. And the person who understands that conversation best is almost never the one with the law degree.

THE UNFAIR ADVANTAGE (AND WHY IT'S STILL NOT ENOUGH)

I'm going to be transparent about something.

Case Connect has access to a source of cases that no other

firm or marketing company in the country can touch. I can't tell you what it is. Not because I'm being coy. Because even if I told you, you couldn't access it. The barrier to entry requires a 1,500-seat call center running around the clock, technology that took years to build, and operational complexity that no single law firm on earth could replicate. We spent tens of millions of dollars building this infrastructure. You can't shortcut your way to it.

But here's the part that should scare you: we have all of that. The best lead sources. The largest advertising dataset in the PI space. The technology. The call center. The infrastructure. And I still watched a firm take everything we gave them and turn $100,000 in perfectly good leads into 5 signed cases. Five. Out of over six hundred leads.

So I took over one single part of their operation. Just one. I didn't change the ads. I didn't change the budget. I didn't change a single thing about the marketing. I changed one variable.

The next month, same spend, we signed 57 cases.

Fifty-seven. Same leads. Same ads. Same hundred grand. One variable changed and the results improved by over 1,000 percent.

I'm going to tell you exactly what that variable was in the next chapter. And when I do, it's going to fundamentally change how you think about every dollar you spend on marketing. Because the truth is, most of you are sitting on a goldmine of leads right now and you're watching them die because of something you've never even thought to fix.

Fifty-seven versus five. Same leads. Same money. One variable.

And when I tell you what it was, it's going to make you sick. Because you've been staring at it every single day and have never seen it.

CHAPTER 3

THE CLOSER (SALES TO ONE)

A HUNDRED THOUSAND DOLLARS. GONE.

That's how it felt. A massive firm came to us. Big operation. Established. Confident. They told us they had everything dialed in on their end. Best intake team in the business. Top-notch staff. World-class process. All they needed was more leads. Just fill the pipeline and we'll take it from here.

So we filled the pipeline.

In one month the ad spend was $100,000. The ads performed beautifully. Over six hundred people who'd been in car accidents picked up their phones, clicked a button, and said: I need help. I'm hurt. I don't know what to do. Please call me.

Six hundred human beings. Scared. In pain. Some of them sitting in hospital parking lots with hands shaking. Some of them lying on their couches with ice packs and neck braces, wondering if they'd ever feel normal again. Some of them crying. All of them waiting for someone to pick up the phone and give a damn.

The firm signed five of them.

Five.

If you've ever poured money into marketing and watched it evaporate, you know the feeling. That sick, hollow pit in your stomach. The spreadsheet that makes you want to close your laptop and walk away. A hundred grand, six hundred real people who raised their hand and asked for help, and almost every single one of them slipped through the cracks. You start questioning everything. Were the leads real? Was the targeting wrong? Did we spend the money in the wrong places? Is marketing just a black hole that eats cash and gives nothing back?

If you've been burned by a marketing company before, you're reading this right now and nodding. You've lived this. You know exactly what this feels like. That knot in your chest. That voice in your head saying: I knew it. Marketing doesn't work. I wasted the money. I should've just stuck with referrals.

But that's not what happened here. And what actually went wrong is going to change the way you think about your entire firm.

I got on a Zoom with this client. Their entire staff was on the call. Think about that meeting for a second. A firm just spent $100,000 with us and signed 5 cases. The owner is furious. His staff is pointing fingers. Everyone on that screen is looking at me like I'm the guy who just lit their money on fire. The tension was so thick you could taste it through a computer screen. Every person on that call wanted someone to blame, and I was the easiest target in the room.

I could have pointed at the data. I could have shown them the lead quality metrics, the opt-in rates, the contact rates. I could have proven that the marketing worked. But nobody on that call wanted to hear about metrics. They wanted to know why $100,000 turned into 5 cases.

So I did something that made my business partner think I'd lost my mind.

I told them: Let me take over your intake for one month. Completely free. Same ads. Same budget. Same leads from the same sources. The only thing that changes is who picks up the phone when it rings. And if you're not happy with the results, I'll comp you the entire ad spend. Every penny. Out of my own pocket.

A hundred thousand dollars of my own money on the line. Because I knew something they didn't. I knew the leads were good. I knew the marketing worked. And I had a gut feeling about what was really broken. I just needed thirty days to prove it.

They said yes. They had nothing to lose. I had everything to lose.

Here's who I put on those phones.

Not attorneys. Not paralegals. Not legal intake specialists with ten years of experience and a stack of certifications. I recruited a group of door-to-door pest control salesmen from the streets of Philadelphia. Kids. Twenty years old. Hungry. Relentless. The kind of young guys who'd knock on a stranger's door in ninety-eight-degree heat and talk their way into a $400 contract before the homeowner even realized what happened. They had crazy energy. They had zero quit. And they had absolutely no idea what a personal injury case was.

Not one of them had ever worked in a law firm. Not one of them knew what a demand letter was. If you asked them the difference between liability and coverage, they'd stare at you like you were speaking Mandarin.

Tyler and I trained them in a week. Seven days. We taught them what an MVA case is. How to qualify one. How to talk to someone who just had the worst day of their life. And then we loaded them up with every piece of sales knowledge I'd accumulated over a decade of selling: the door-to-door grind as a kid, the gym memberships sold across from people in tears, the Mercedes deals closed on the showroom floor, the instinct you only build by sitting across from thousands of real people and learning what makes them trust you. All of it. Compressed into seven days and poured into these kids like rocket fuel.

Then we turned the phones on.

Same leads. Same ads. Same hundred thousand dollars.

Fifty-seven signed cases.

Fifty-seven cases signed by kids who'd never read a retainer in their lives. Five signed by the professionals. The best attorney in that room never signed a single one.

I need you to let that sink in. Same pool of people. Same injuries. Same fear, same confusion, same desperation. The leads weren't bad. The marketing wasn't broken. Not a single thing about the advertising changed. The only difference was the voice on the other end of the line. Kids from Philly with a week of training outperformed a "world-class" legal intake team by over 1,000 percent.

The marketing was never the problem. It was never the leads. It was never the budget or the targeting or the platforms. It was the people answering the phone. It was intake. And the firm had no idea because they were so convinced their team was the best in the business that they never bothered to question it.

The owner called me. His voice was different from the first time we spoke. Quieter. He said: "I'm willing to admit when I'm wrong." He handed us the account. It's one of our largest to this day, and we've done great business together for years.

But this story isn't about Case Connect. It's about a truth that should make every attorney reading this book put down their coffee and stare at the wall.

Your intake is almost certainly broken. And the reason you don't know it is because you've never seen what it looks like when it's not.

THE PAMPHLET WITH A LAW DEGREE

Here's what the firm's original team was doing on those calls. And I'd bet my house that your team is doing the same thing right now.

They answered the phone the way you'd answer a form at the DMV. Name. Date of accident. Were you injured? Is there a police report? Do you have insurance? Great, we're going to send over some documents, take a look and get back to us.

Click.

No warmth. No curiosity. No attempt to understand the trembling voice on the other end. The caller just told them that an eighteen-wheeler ran a red light and T-boned them at forty-five miles per hour, and the response was: "Okay. And what's your date of birth?"

They weren't having a conversation. They were conducting a deposition. Checking boxes on a screen while a human being on the other end was silently begging someone to care. These people just went through one of the most traumatic experiences of their lives, and they called your firm looking for a lifeline. What they got instead was a pamphlet with a law degree. Cold. Transactional. Forgettable.

And here's the part that really burns: Your team thinks they're good at this. They've been doing it for years. They have a "process." They'll tell you they're closing everything that comes through the door. Ask them for the actual number and watch what happens. They'll either give you a number that would make me shut down my company and come work for them, or they'll change the subject. Either way, they've never tracked it. They have no idea what their real conversion rate is. They're guessing at the one metric that determines whether your firm lives or dies.

And you want to know who's feeding them this delusion? Their own staff. So many firms have in-house marketing teams whose entire job, whether they realize it or not, is to prove why every outside source doesn't work. The leads are bad. The cases are junk. The marketing company is a scam. They spend more energy building a case against their own lead sources than they do actually calling the leads. And the attorneys believe them. Meanwhile, that same team can't tell you their cost per case, claims they convert 95 percent of their leads, and the firm is out here shopping for lead gen companies. If you're converting 95 percent, why are you looking for more leads? Something doesn't add up.

My guy John has been with us since day one. He gets on Zoom calls with firms like this all the time. One call, a California firm, their entire staff on the screen, and they're going down the list telling John that the leads are spam. Nobody picks up. The numbers are fake. They've tried calling and nobody answers. They were proud of it. Like they'd caught us red-handed.

John pulled up one of the leads they'd marked as spam. Right there on the Zoom. Dialed the number. One ring. The person picked up. John ran the intake live, right in front of the entire staff, and signed the case on the spot. A lead the firm swore was fake. Signed. In real time. While they watched.

Nobody on that Zoom said a word.

The legal industry got fat. It got lazy. For decades, firms never had to compete for clients. People just showed up. The phone rang. Cases walked through the door. Nobody had to sell. Nobody had to connect. Nobody had to fight for the person on the other end of the line. And now, in a world where every lead is being fought over by six firms, a dozen marketing companies, and a handful of illegal runners, that laziness isn't just a bad habit. It's a death sentence.

The firms that treat intake as a sales function will eat. The firms that keep treating it like paperwork will starve. It really is that binary.

THE OBJECTION YOU NEVER HEARD

Here's something almost nobody in this industry talks about, and it's the single biggest reason you're losing cases you should be signing.

Picture this. Your team does the intake. Gathers all the information. Qualifies the case. Everything checks out. Then your rep says some version of: "Great, I'm going to send you the retainer agreement. Take a look, and if everything looks good, sign it and send it back."

You know what happens next. About 25 percent of those people actually sign. The other 75 percent vanish. They don't answer your calls. They don't respond to emails. They ghost you. And you tell yourself they weren't serious, or they went with another firm, or they "weren't ready."

But none of that is what happened.

When that person said "I'll look it over and get back to you," here's what they were actually telling you: I don't trust you yet. I'm just too polite to say it to your face.

That's not a timing problem. That's not a "bad lead" problem. That's a trust problem. And your process created it by jumping to the close before the person ever felt certain that *you* were the right choice. You skipped straight from collecting information to "sign here" without ever building the bridge between their pain and your solution. So they took the documents, sat at home with every doubt still swirling in their head, and never opened them.

And even if they do sign? Remember those four MVA ads out of nine posts I saw scrolling Instagram? Your client saw them too. The second they hang up, their phone rings. Another firm. Then another. Then a text. Then a DM. They don't know you from the next attorney any more than they know one billboard from another. If you didn't create deep, emotional certainty on that call, if you just collected info and sent paperwork, they'll sign with the next person who actually makes them feel heard. Or worse, some runner shows up at their door with a pitch and a smile and you never hear from them again.

And here's something we haven't even gotten to yet. Even after you sign the client, the war isn't over. Not even close. But I'll get to that later.

The framework I'm about to show you eliminates this. It surfaces every objection. It handles every doubt. It creates absolute certainty *before* you ever present a single document. By the time the retainer hits their screen, signing it isn't a decision. It's a formality.

SPEED KILLS (IN YOUR FAVOR)

Before I break down the framework, you need to understand something about timing that will change how you think about every lead that's ever come through your door.

If you call a lead within sixty seconds of them opting in, you are 81 percent more likely to convert them. Eighty-one percent. Just from being fast.

That number drops off a cliff with every minute. By five minutes, you've lost more than half your advantage. By thirty minutes, that lead has already talked to three other firms, gotten confused, had second thoughts, or decided to "deal with it later." By the time your paralegal gets around to checking the inbox after lunch, that person is someone else's client.

Every minute of delay is money walking out your door and into your competitor's pocket.

Our rep Jason signed a case the other day that still blows my mind. The guy was standing on the side of the road. Accident had just happened. Police hadn't even arrived yet. He was waiting for the cops, scrolling his phone, hit one of our ads, and filled out the form. Jason was on the line with him before the squad car pulled up. Signed him right there at the scene. Walked him through every step while he stood next to his wrecked car waiting for a tow truck. By the time the police report was filed, that man was already represented.

Fifteen minutes. From accident to signed client. That's what speed looks like when the system is built for it.

Here's what happens on our end. A lead comes in from an ad. It hits our system. AI verifies it's legitimate in real time. It routes to our call center. Within thirty seconds, the phone is ringing. Not thirty minutes. Thirty seconds. We run a massive tech dialer that can process thousands of lines simultaneously. Our reps are always live, always ready, always on the line with qualified cases.

The person who just got into an accident and submitted their information is talking to a trained, hungry, empathetic human being before they've even set their phone down from filling out the form.

Can your firm do that? Be honest.

If the answer is no, that's not a character flaw. It's a capacity problem. And it's fixable. But you have to stop pretending your current process is working when your own numbers are screaming that it's not.

I want to show you what it actually sounds like when intake is done right. Not as a list of steps. As a real conversation. Because the difference between a firm that signs 5 cases and a firm that signs 57 from the same leads isn't a checklist. It's what happens between two human beings on a phone call.

The phone rings. One of our reps picks up. On the other end is a woman named Maria. She's thirty-eight. She was rear-ended at a stoplight three days ago. Her neck is killing her. She hasn't slept. She can't turn her head to check on her kids in the back seat when she drives, which terrifies her, so she stopped driving. Her husband has been picking up extra shifts to cover the Uber rides and the medical copays. She filled out a form online at 11:00 p.m. last night because she couldn't sleep and didn't know what else to do.

Here's how most firms handle Maria.

"Hi Maria, thanks for reaching out. I'm going to ask you a few questions. When did the accident happen? Was a police report filed? Were you at fault? Do you have insurance? Okay, great. I'm going to send you some documents to review. Take a look and give us a call back if you'd like to move forward."

Maria hangs up. She feels nothing. She learned nothing. She's no more confident than she was before the call. The documents sit in her email unopened. Another firm calls her the next day, and that rep actually listens, and Maria signs with them instead.

Your firm never hears from her again. You chalk it up to a "bad lead."

Now here's how our team handles Maria.

"Hey Maria, this is Chris with [firm]. I'm calling because you submitted some information about an accident. First, I just want to make sure you're okay. I'm going to ask you a few quick questions to see if we can help, and if everything checks out, I'll walk you through exactly what we can do. Sound good?"

Sixty seconds. Chris has set the tone. Maria knows who he is, why he's calling, and what she's going to get out of this. She's not confused. She's not anxious. She feels like someone is in control and that person is there for *her*.

Chris qualifies. Fault. Treatment. Date of loss. Insurance. He confirms it's a real case. Then he shifts gears.

"Maria, you mentioned your neck has been hurting since the accident. When you say hurting, what does that feel like for you specifically?"

Silence. Then she tells him. It's a sharp, burning pain that starts at the base of her skull and radiates down into her shoulders. She can't turn her head. She tried to pick up her two-year-old last Tuesday and almost dropped him because the pain shot down her arm.

"My God, I'm so sorry. That sounds awful. How is that showing up in the rest of your life right now? What's changed since the accident?"

Now the walls come down.

She tells him everything. She can't drive. Her husband is working doubles. She feels guilty because her kids are confused about why mommy won't pick them up anymore. She's scared the pain might be permanent. She hasn't been back to the doctor because she doesn't know how she'll pay for it. She starts crying. Not because Chris manipulated her. Because nobody had asked her these questions. Nobody had given her the space to say it out loud. She'd been holding all of it inside for three days, and this stranger on the phone was the first person who actually wanted to know.

Chris talks less than 30 percent of the time. He's not lecturing. He's not listing credentials. He's asking questions and steering the conversation with empathy. He's in control, but Maria feels like she's driving. That's the illusion. Maria doesn't know what needs to happen to determine if she has a case. Chris does. He never surrenders the wheel. Because giving up control isn't being polite. It's failing the injured person who called you for help.

Now Chris widens the gap.

"Maria, let me make sure I understand what you're dealing with. You've got a neck injury that's keeping you from driving, from picking up your kids, from sleeping. Your husband is working overtime to cover the costs. And you haven't been able to get the treatment you need because you're worried about paying for it. Does that sound right?"

Maria says yes. Quietly. Like hearing it reflected back made it more real.

"Here's what I need you to understand. When people try to handle this on their own, it gets worse. If you don't get proper treatment now, the insurance company will use that against you. They call it a gap in treatment, and they'll argue that if you were really hurt, you would've seen a doctor. They'll use it to deny your claim entirely. Does that make sense?"

"Yes." Her voice is smaller now.

"And here's the scary part. Just because your neck feels like a seven out of ten right now doesn't mean it stays there. Injuries from accidents like yours show up weeks, sometimes months later. Something that feels manageable today turns into a herniated disc or nerve damage down the road. And when that happens, if there's a gap in your treatment records, insurance will deny everything. You'll be stuck paying for surgeries, therapy, all of it, out of your own pocket, for an accident that wasn't your fault. Does that make sense?"

Maria is quiet. She's seeing a future she hadn't considered.

Chris does it again from a different angle. The lost wages. The mounting bills. The stress on her marriage. Each time: "Does that make sense? Do you agree?" Micro-commitments. He's not building a legal case. He's building the case inside Maria's own mind that doing nothing is the most dangerous option on the table.

"Based on everything we just talked about, all the issues you're dealing with and what we covered about how this can go sideways if it's not handled, do you feel confident that getting the right team in your corner is the best move for you right now?"

Maria says yes. Because by now, saying no would mean ignoring everything she just agreed was true.

Now, Chris gives her the *how*.

"Here's exactly what we're going to do for you. We're going to get you connected with a medical team that specializes in accident injuries so your neck gets treated properly. We're going to handle the insurance company so you don't have to deal with them. You don't pay a dime out of pocket. And we're going to fight to make sure you're compensated for everything you've been through. The missed work. The pain. All of it. How does that sound?"

Maria signs. On the call. Right then. Not "I'll send you the documents." Not "take a look and get back to us." She signs because every objection was handled before the retainer ever appeared on her screen. There's nothing left to think about. The decision was made three minutes ago.

And then Chris does one more thing that most firms would never think to do.

"Maria, I want to give you a heads up. Over the next few days, you're going to get calls from other law firms. They'll tell you they can get you more money. They'll tell you to switch. It happens to everyone. Here's what you need to know: You already have the best team on this. We're already working on your case. If anyone calls, just tell them you're represented and hang up. Don't engage. We've got you."

That's the defensive wall. Without it, you're sending a signed client into a war zone wearing a paper gown. Other firms are calling. Runners are knocking on doors. Texts are flooding in. If you don't inoculate the client against it before you hang up, someone else will peel them away before the ink on the retainer is dry.

That's the call. That's what 57 out of 600 looks like instead of 5. Same Maria. Same injury. Same fear. The only difference is whether the person who answers the phone treats her like a case number or a human being.

WHEN THE FIRM BLOWS IT

I have to tell you something that still makes me sick to my stomach.

We signed a case. The whole system worked perfectly. Lead came in. Our rep connected with the caller. Built the pain. Found the nerve. Handled every objection. Closed it. Set the wall. The client felt heard, felt safe, felt taken care of for the first time since her accident.

Then we live-transferred her to the firm for onboarding.

The woman who answered the phone at the firm sounded like she was working the drive-through window at a McDonald's on a Tuesday afternoon. Annoyed. Miserable. Like the call was an interruption to whatever she was actually doing. The client, who five minutes earlier had tears in her eyes as she told our rep that she couldn't pick up her daughter because of her back, was suddenly being treated like a number on a spreadsheet.

She hung up. And never answered the phone again.

We tried everything to save it. But when someone goes from feeling understood and cared for to being treated like an inconvenience in the span of a phone transfer, the trust doesn't just crack. It shatters. They're done. They'll sign with the next person who makes them feel like a human being.

This happens more often than you'd think. We've fired clients over it. Firms that consistently destroy the experience we built for the caller don't get to work with us. Because every client who gets mistreated on a handoff doesn't just cost that firm one case. It damages the reputation we've spent years building. And I will not allow that.

If you're reading this thinking, *That's not my firm*, I hope you're right. But when's the last time you actually listened to how your staff answers the phone? Not what you imagine they sound like. What they actually sound like to a scared, injured person reaching out for help at the lowest point of their life.

You might be horrified.

THE MACHINE THAT SEES EVERYTHING

I need to tell you about something we built. I can't give you the full story yet because it deserves its own chapter. But what I'm about to describe should make every hair on the back of your neck stand up.

We built an AI platform called AYRA Legal. Every single intake call that runs through our system gets analyzed in real time. The AI listens. It scores. It identifies where things went right, where things went wrong, and it catches things that no human being on earth would ever notice.

One example that still gives me chills. A rep lost a catastrophic injury case during intake. Massive case. The kind that settles for seven figures. The caller read through the retainer and got caught on a clause about owing money back if the case didn't win. The rep froze. Didn't know how to handle it. The caller said, "Let me think about it" and hung up. AYRA flagged the call instantly. It pulled the exact moment the objection hit. It wrote a summary of the issue. And it told a manager, word for word, exactly what to say to call back and close the case. The manager picked up the phone. Explained the clause. The client signed. That seven-figure case, the kind you build a year around, was two minutes from walking out the door forever. Our AI caught it. A human never would have.

That's not software. That's a weapon. And I'll tell you the full story of how I built it in the next chapter. In a bathroom. With a Surface Pro propped up against the wall. Running on three hours of sleep. It nearly destroyed my marriage, and it might be the most important thing I've ever created.

WHAT YOU'RE ACTUALLY LOSING

Here's the part that should keep you up tonight.

Think about last month. Think about every lead that came into your firm. Every phone call. Every form submission. Every person who reached out because they were hurt and needed help. Now ask yourself: How many of them became clients?

Not how many you think you converted. Not the number your intake team told you. The real number.

You don't know it. I already know you don't. Because nobody does. Nobody tracks it. Nobody measures how many leads came in, how many were contacted, how many were lost, and where they went. The numbers that determine whether your firm lives or dies are sitting in a black hole somewhere between your phone system and your case management software, and you're guessing at all of them.

The reality is brutal. Most firms convert between 5 percent and 10 percent of their leads. That means for every hundred people who reach out to your firm, ninety of them sign with someone else. Ninety people who needed *your* help. Ninety cases that could have been *your* revenue. Gone.

Now think about what we did with the same leads. Five cases became fifty-seven. By changing one thing.

If you're spending $20,000 a month on marketing right now and converting at 8 percent, you're signing eight cases. There are ninety-two other people who called your firm, told you they were hurt, and never became your clients. At $18,000 average fee per case, those ninety-two lost opportunities represent $1.6 million in revenue. Every month. Walking out your door because the person who answered the phone treated the call like a trip to the DMV instead of the most important conversation of that person's day.

I walked an attorney through that math on a Zoom once. Shared my screen. Typed the numbers into a calculator in real time so he could watch them multiply. When I hit enter on the final number, his camera might as well have frozen. He just sat there. Ten seconds of nothing. Then, quietly, almost to himself: "That can't be right." It was right. He knew it was right. He just didn't want to calculate how many years he'd been bleeding at that rate without knowing it.

Fix your intake. Double your conversion. Same ad spend. Same leads. That's $1.7 million in additional annual revenue without spending a single extra dollar on marketing.

Or keep sending retainers and praying 25 percent come back signed. Your call.

Here's what I know about you right now.

Part of you is fired up. You can see it. This isn't that complicated. Fix the intake. Train the team. Stop treating the most important conversation in your firm like an afterthought. You can start tomorrow morning.

Good. Everything I just showed you is real and actionable. The framework. The questions. The psychology. None of it requires a 1,500-seat call center or AI software. It requires discipline, empathy, and a willingness to treat every single intake call like the $18,000 conversation it actually is.

But there's a quieter voice. And it's saying: "I'd need to hire closers. Train them. Manage them. Buy a dialer. Build the infrastructure. Monitor every call. And I went to law school to practice law, not run a sales floor."

That voice isn't wrong. The best intake reps in this country make $150,000 to $200,000 a year because they're worth it. A great closer signing 10 extra cases a month is generating $180,000 in revenue for your firm. But finding them, training them, paying them, and building the tech stack around them is a full-time operation on top of your law practice.

Either way, the leads aren't going to wait. Right now, at this very moment, someone is filling out a form to find a personal injury attorney. The question is whether that person becomes your client or someone else's. And the answer depends entirely on what happens in the first sixty seconds after they hit submit.

But signing cases is only half the equation. Because once the cases start flowing, a whole new set of problems shows up. Problems that nearly destroyed everything I built.

A few months after everything clicked, after the cases were flowing and the machine was humming and I thought I finally had it figured out, I was sitting in my office staring at a fifty-seven-inch ultrawide monitor. A P&L was on the screen. The accountant's voice was in my ear, but it had become noise. Not signal. Just a low drone I could hear but couldn't process, because the number staring back at me through those pixels had emptied every thought from my head.

Eight hundred thousand dollars in losses. One month.

And that was just the beginning.

CHAPTER 4

THE ARCHITECT (SYSTEMS THAT SCALE)

I WAS ON THE PHONE WITH MY ACCOUNTANT WHEN THE floor dropped out.

He'd been raising alarms for weeks. Something wasn't right with the numbers. But we'd been changing so many things at once that he couldn't point to the source. It was like a giant ship taking on water with two tiny holes in different locations, and every time he tried to trace the leak, the water shifted.

Every time he called, I brushed it off. Annoyed. Dismissive. I kept telling myself it was unearned revenue. Payments that came in last month for services we were delivering this month. Timing. Accounting noise. Normal stuff. I didn't want to hear it because hearing it would mean something was wrong with the people I'd just put in charge. And admitting that would mean I'd made the wrong call.

I was in denial. And denial is the most expensive emotion a business owner can afford.

Let me back up.

Case Connect was doing $26 million a year, and I was killing myself. I was the marketing department, the sales floor, the billing team, and the CEO. All at once. Every morning I woke up ready for war. Emails, ads, sales calls, pipeline reviews, Slack huddles, attorney calls, mid-day fires, end-of-day fires, fires I didn't even know were burning until I smelled the smoke. I was pulling information out of my team's heads through nonstop meetings because there was no system to surface it automatically. Everything lived in people's brains or in scattered spreadsheets that nobody updated.

I felt like a firefighter with houses burning on every block, armed with nothing but a garden hose. My body was breaking down. Losing weight. Snapping at my kids over nothing. Coming home, physically present but mentally gone. I was doing everything, and nothing was getting done the way it should have been.

So I made the decision that every burned-out founder eventually makes. I hired help.

A CMO from a well-known agency. He was supposed to systematize and build out the marketing department so I could step back and do CEO things. And a VP of Sales. My neighbor. Our daughters were best friends. He'd come from JG Wentworth, where he'd supposedly built their entire sales operation. He was supposed to see the opportunity and figure out how to make it happen.

Their combined salary was north of $400,000 a year.

WHEN IMPRESSIVE ISN'T ENOUGH

The CMO's first week looked like a revelation. He put together a complete game plan. Organized every campaign into Asana. Made every team member log their changes, document their tasks, track their work. Structure. Accountability. Order. For the first time, the marketing department looked like it had a brain. I sat back and thought: This is the guy. This is what I've been missing.

I was fired up. I let myself believe.

Then the cracks started. He "needed" hires I didn't agree with. Overseas reps doing work I couldn't see the value in. I watched him shift budgets between campaigns, and my gut twisted because the moves felt wrong. Too many changes, too fast. I'd spent years building instinct about which campaigns to feed and which to starve. He was rearranging the whole thing like a guy reorganizing someone else's kitchen. Efficient looking. But everything was in the wrong drawer.

I bit my tongue. Everyone tells you not to micromanage. Give them the what, let them figure out the how. Empower them or you'll ruin them. So I watched decisions being made that didn't sit right, decisions I wouldn't have made, and I let them go because maybe he knew something I didn't.

Every time I asked for reporting, I got the same answer. Things are too unorganized. He can't get me the numbers I need. The infrastructure isn't there yet. Weeks turned into months, and I still didn't have a dashboard. I still didn't have real-time data. He was flying blind and blaming the plane.

Meanwhile, the VP of Sales was losing control of the floor. I started noticing things. Reps not showing up on time. Numbers that didn't add up. Major clients going unanswered. The director of intake, a guy who'd been solid, abruptly quit a few weeks after the VP came onboard. He never said why. He just left. I think he saw the direction things were heading and wanted no part of it. The VP wasn't leading from the front. He never got on the phones. Never jumped in and helped his people close deals. He sat buried in spreadsheets analyzing random data while his team drifted. Numbers can't solve everything. Sometimes you just have to roll up your sleeves, get on the floor, and lead from the front lines.

Here's what I didn't understand then, but I do now. There is a massive difference between someone who built something as an employee at a company that already had infrastructure, funding, and support, and someone who can figure things out from scratch. One is a magician. The other is a bowler with gutter guards up. The VP ran a playbook at JG Wentworth. But running someone else's playbook in someone else's building with someone else's resources is a completely different skill than looking at chaos and creating order out of nothing. At Case Connect, there were no gutter guards. And without them, the ball went straight into the gutter.

I stepped back. Everyone says don't micromanage. So I tried to write this book instead. That's why it took so long to finish.

For about sixty days, I trusted that the machine was running. I wasn't watching the dashboard because I'd hired people to watch it for me. I didn't have real-time reporting because nobody had built it. I didn't have automated alerts because the systems hadn't been built yet. I was flying blind and didn't know it.

Then the accountant called. Then the P&L landed on my screen.

I was sitting in my office. Fluorescent light humming above me, baking the top of my head. Giant monitor in front of me with a P&L that looked like it had been written in a foreign language. I kept scrolling, looking for something familiar, something I could grab onto and make sense of. The numbers should have added up. They didn't.

We spent $800,000 more on marketing than we brought in from clients. In a single month. Eight hundred thousand dollars.

Gone. Not spread across a quarter. Not a cumulative loss that built slowly over time. One month. One P&L. One number that made me want to throw up.

My stomach dropped. I got nauseous. I stood up and paced around my office in a haze, that kind of pacing where your legs are moving but your brain hasn't caught up yet. The kids were at school. The nanny had the baby. The house was dead quiet. And the silence screamed at me.

The losses weren't all in one place. That's what made it so hard to catch. A campaign here burning $3,000 a day on leads that weren't even making it into our dialer. A conversion rate there that had cratered because nobody was watching the intake floor. Small leaks in random locations. None of them big enough to trigger an alarm on their own. All of them together: $2 million in net losses.

Two million dollars. Because I took my eyes off the road for sixty days.

And then I found the worst part.

After both of them were gone, after I'd taken everything back and started combing through the wreckage, I discovered a nationwide campaign the CMO had been running. Over $1.1 million in ad spend. Unaccounted for. Every lead from that campaign went out the door. Cases generated and delivered to attorneys. Revenue that should have come back to us. None of it tracked. None of it billed. Over a million dollars in spend that didn't appear on a single report because nobody logged it. He'd been running it to supplement the poor performance of everything else, papering over the holes with volume that we were paying for and never getting paid back for.

A million-point-one in ghost spend. That was the moment I stopped being angry and started being scared.

What happened next was slow and ugly. I started taking things back. Piece by piece. Looking over shoulders. Asking questions I shouldn't have needed to ask. When I lose faith in people, I can't sit back. I start doing things for them. I hop into meetings and take over. I tell them what to do instead of waiting for them to figure it out. And once that starts, it's over. The trust is gone.

The VP sent a text one morning. Early. He was done. I responded, thanked him, and wished him the best. The CMO resigned right after our head media buyer under him resigned. Things got tough and everyone bailed. But it only got tough because the people who bailed were the ones who broke it.

When they left, I did all their jobs. And things weren't tough anymore. They were way better. We started the year at negative $2 million in EBITDA. They left in April. By year-end, we were above $5 million. Do the math on that. Starting in May at negative two, and ending the year at positive five. That's how fast I dug us out. And that's how much damage they were doing every day they were in the building.

But here's the thing about me that I've learned to accept. I thrive in turmoil. When everything is burning and the odds say you can't possibly make it through, something clicks on inside me that doesn't exist when things are smooth. I sat down with a journal, and I wrote things that would scare a normal person. How I was going to burn the world down to make this work. How nobody was going to stop me. One-man wolfpack.

My wife looked at me during the worst of it and said: "You always make things work. It'll be fine."

She didn't get it. Not really. I was always fine. I always made it work. Nothing ever got to me. And that was the problem. She'd never seen me scared before because I'd never let her. But I was. For the first time in my career, I was terrified down to my bones. Not of the money. But of what losing it meant for the people who depended on me. Every employee with a mortgage. Every family counting on a paycheck from a company that was hemorrhaging cash.

But her confidence did something to me. It reminded me that fear is just a feeling. And feelings don't fix P&Ls. Work does.

I fired the staff that the old regime had poisoned. Cycled in fresh blood. Rallied the team. Promised them I wouldn't let a single person fail. And I didn't. Within three weeks, lead costs stabilized. Cost per case came back in line. Conversion rates returned to where they should have been. Within thirty days, we were profitable again.

And the whole time, one thought was eating me alive.

I shouldn't have needed thirty days. I should have caught it in week one. If I'd had reporting. If I'd had dashboards. If I'd had a system that surfaced the numbers before they became a crisis, I would have seen the $3,000-a-day campaign bleeding out on day two. Not month two. I would have seen the conversion rates dropping before they cost me seven figures. I would have seen the iceberg before the ship hit it.

I didn't have any of that. And it cost me $2 million and nearly cost me everything else.

THE ICEBERG IN THE DARK

Here's what I need you to hear.

If you're running a personal injury firm right now and you can't tell me your cost per case, your conversion rate, your lead volume by source, and your revenue per client type without looking it up, you are me before that P&L showed up on my screen. You're flying the plane with no instruments. No altimeter. No fuel gauge. No radar. You're relying on the feeling of the ride to tell you whether you're climbing or falling. And by the time you feel the dive, it's too late.

Most attorneys live here. They find out they're in trouble when the bank account looks thin. When payroll is tight. When the pipeline feels slow. Those are lagging indicators. They tell you what already happened. By the time you're looking at a bank statement wondering where the money went, the money has been gone for weeks.

You need leading indicators. Numbers that tell you what's *about* to happen. Cost per lead this week versus last week. Contact rates by day. Conversion rates by rep. Spend by campaign with real-time return data. These numbers are the sonar that shows you the iceberg while it's still three miles out.

Without them, you're the Titanic. And you won't feel the impact until you're already sinking.

THE ONE RULE

Somewhere in the chaos of rebuilding after the $2 million loss, I had a conversation with one of my developers about why people couldn't seem to follow directions. I was frustrated. Things I'd explained clearly were being done wrong. Steps were getting skipped. Details were falling through cracks. I couldn't understand why.

He said something that stuck: "The things that are obvious to you aren't obvious to anyone else. That's why you're you and they're them. If they could think the way you do, they'd be running their own company."

He was right. And it changed how I built everything from that point forward.

The rule became simple: If I had to explain something more than once, it needed to be documented. Period. No exceptions.

My oldest daughter Aria had a soccer game one Saturday. Soccer Shots. She was young, still shy, and half the time she stood at the edge of the field watching the other kids instead of joining in. I was supposed to be there for her. Instead I was on the sideline with my phone, writing a Google Doc for a billing process that my team had botched twice. I could see her out of the corner of my eye, not participating, standing by herself. And I could feel her noticing me not watching. I tried to hide the fact that I'd noticed her noticing. Tried to pretend I was only glancing at the phone. But kids see everything. They always do. And the worst part wasn't that I missed the game. It was that I tried to hide from myself the fact that I was choosing a Google Doc over my daughter. Instead of putting the phone down, walking over, and kneeling next to her and helping her feel brave enough to join, I documented a billing workflow.

That's the tax. That's what building a company costs you when you don't have systems. You end up writing processes on the sideline of your kid's soccer game because nobody else can do what lives in your head. And every minute you spend being the system is a minute stolen from the people who need you to be a person.

I recorded myself doing billing processes at midnight. Kitchen counter. All the lights off. No shirt, just shorts. Talking into a Loom in a hushed voice so I didn't wake my wife and kids, walking through each step so that any new hire could execute it without asking me a single question. I broke everything down to a fifth-grade level. Not because my team was stupid. Because clarity is kindness. The people who think they're too smart to write simple instructions are the same people who end up doing everything themselves because nobody can follow their genius-level explanations. That's not leadership. That's ego. And ego doesn't scale.

I deconstructed our entire client onboarding process the same way Toyota builds a car. Sales completes their tasks, hands to billing. Billing completes their tasks, hands to IT. IT completes their tasks, hands back to sales. Sales does a quality check, notifies the client, moves them to live. Every step documented. Every handoff defined. Every checkpoint built in.

If you're an attorney reading this, you already have processes. You just haven't written them down. Your intake has steps. Your case management has steps. Your demand letter process has steps. They live in your head, or in the heads of one or two people on your team, and when those people leave or get sick or make a mistake, the whole thing collapses.

Write it down. Record it. Make it foolproof. And then inspect what you expect. Because processes get tweaked, skipped, and changed the second you stop watching. Especially when you grow and introduce new people. A system is only as good as the last time someone verified it was actually being followed.

This is how you stop being the bottleneck. Not by hiring expensive executives and hoping they figure it out. By documenting the machine so that anyone can run it, and then building the technology to make sure it's running right. The best attorney in the world can't outwork a system that runs while they sleep. And the attorney who tries to *be* the system will always lose to the one who builds it.

Which brings me to the most important thing I've ever built.

THE WEAPON I BUILT IN A SHOWER

AYRA Legal started as a simple idea. An AI that could listen to intake calls in real time and tell reps what to sign and what to pass on. So an intake rep would never lose a good case because they had to pause and verify with an attorney. And they'd never sign a bad case that would earn the firm a terrible review.

That was it. A call-scoring tool. Something narrow and specific.

But once I started building the framework, the idea wouldn't stop growing. If the AI could analyze calls for case quality, it could analyze them for rep performance. If it could score rep performance, it could cross-reference that data against the marketing source that generated the lead. If it could see marketing and intake together, it could tell you which campaigns to scale and which to kill. It could tell you which reps were bleeding leads and why. It could replace the CMO who cost me $200,000 a year and couldn't point to a single metric that mattered.

Every layer I added revealed another layer underneath it. The idea consumed me.

For two or three weeks, I disappeared.

I don't mean I was busy. I mean I ceased to exist as a functioning human being. My laptop was open in my center console while I drove on cruise control down the highway. I sat at my daughters' friends' birthday parties in the corner, headphones in, typing on my laptop while other parents watched their kids play and probably wondered what was wrong with me. I went to family parties and sat in a corner, ignoring everyone. My eyes burned from the screen. My heart raced from the coffee and the adrenaline and the feeling that I was building something that nobody had ever built before.

I used voice-to-text in the shower with my Surface Pro propped against the wall outside the glass. People who know me aren't surprised by this. I take calls on my AirPods in the shower. I eat lunch on Zoom. I've bathed my kids with a laptop open on the bathroom counter, running a meeting with the camera off while I scrub shampoo out of someone's hair. That's how I'm wired. When something grabs me, I can't let go. I physically cannot think about anything else until it's done.

I barely ate. Went days without a real meal. Skipped workouts for the first time in years. Ignored calls and texts from people I cared about. Slept five hours a night, which for some-one who's neurotic about getting eight, felt like running on fumes.

I told my wife: "You're not going to see me for a few days."

She looked at me. She'd seen this version of me before. I pulled up the screen and tried to explain what I was building. How it would give me visibility into everything. How it would make sure the $2 million loss could never happen again. How it would change our entire business.

She looked at me like I was speaking a foreign language. She nodded. She pretended to understand. And then she did what she always does: She cleared the path. Took care of the kids. Held down the house. Gave me the space to disappear into the work. She was supportive to a point. But she also needed me. My kids needed me. And I wasn't there. Not really. I was in the room but I was gone. She couldn't understand why I couldn't just pause for twenty minutes and be present. But that's not how my brain works. When I'm locked in, the world outside the screen stops existing.

Every logic tree and decision path I'd spent years building, every instinct I'd developed about what to scale, what to kill, and who was dropping the ball, I fed into a machine that could execute it twenty-four hours a day with no ego, no bad days, and no $400,000 salary.

Then one morning, it worked.

I was in my office. Alone. The screen in front of me was a dark-mode spreadsheet. Rows and columns of campaign data glowing white and green against a black background. I watched the prototype pace our campaigns against our clients' budgets in real time. I watched it flag a campaign that had spent a few thousand dollars and generated almost no leads. Before AYRA, that campaign might have burned money for weeks before anyone noticed. AYRA caught it on day one. But it didn't just catch it. It went deeper. It realized the leads from that campaign weren't even posting to our dialer. We were paying for leads that were vanishing into thin air. The AI found the leak, turned off the spend, and surfaced the technical issue. All of it. Automatically.

I called my developer. I was pacing between my office and my home gym, the same loop I always walk when my brain is running too fast for my legs to keep up. I'd just had my third coffee, and my heart was pounding. I was ratcheting my fidget spinner in my free hand, the way I always do when the adrenaline is too much for my body to hold still.

"Dude. This is working. Do you understand what just happened? We just saved sixty thousand dollars."

He laughed. "Yeah man, that's what it was supposed to do."

He was right. But he didn't live the losses. He didn't watch $2 million evaporate because nobody could see the leaks. He didn't sit in that office under fluorescent lights staring at a P&L that made him want to throw up. That's why it hit me differently. That's why I called Tyler and my wife and everyone I could think of to tell them what had just happened.

I named it AYRA. After my daughters, Aria and Ayla. It wasn't just a name. It was a reminder. Without this kind of visibility, I was risking everything. Not just the business. Their future. Their security. Every person who works for me has kids and a mortgage and a family that depends on them showing up to a company that's healthy. My decisions impact all of their lives. AYRA was the tool that would make sure I never flew blind again. That I'd see the icebergs in the dark and steer around them. That the ship would reach its destination with everyone on board.

My wife will find out what the name means when she reads this book.

Within weeks, AYRA was catching things I hadn't even designed it to catch.

I was at my desk midday, bouncing between Slack threads and a campaign review, when a notification popped. AYRA had detected a pattern buried in our data that no human would have found in a thousand hours of staring at spreadsheets: a disproportionate number of high-value commercial vehicle cases were coming from one specific campaign that nobody was paying attention to. Hidden in a sea of thousands of campaigns and tens of thousands of leads, this one vein of gold was sitting there quietly producing monsters. AYRA flagged it. Told us to scale the spend. We did. One of the cases that came through that scaled campaign became one of the biggest we'd ever touched. Without that alert, it walks out the door and we never know it existed.

Then it found something bigger. The day after AYRA identified an 84 percent drop-off at a single point in one of our survey funnels, I was in the car on my way to look at a shore property. My wife was driving. I pulled out my phone and opened the dashboard.

The drop-off was at 44 percent.

One day. One suggestion from the AI. One change to the wording of a single question in a survey funnel. And nearly half the people we'd been losing came back. I stared at that number on my phone screen while the shore houses blurred past the window, and I thought: *This is what it was supposed to feel like. This is what visibility looks like.*

The day before, eighty-four out of every one hundred people quit at the same spot in our process. A human analyst might have noticed eventually. AYRA didn't just notice it. It analyzed the question, identified why it was killing conversions, and told us exactly how to reframe it. We made the change. And now I was sitting in a passenger seat watching the results update in real time on a device that fit in my palm.

That's the power. Not that it's smart. That it molds to you. I can see my business anywhere, any time. Sitting in my office at 6:00 a.m. or riding shotgun on the way to the shore. If something is off, I know before anyone else does. It operates twenty-four hours a day. No bad days. No distractions. No resignation letter the same week as the other executive.

My weekly review takes thirty minutes. Everything I need to know about the health of my entire operation, on one screen. If something is outside expected ranges, AYRA doesn't just flag it. It tells me why and what to do about it. Even if I step away for a week, the machine is watching.

Thirty minutes. That's the difference between flying blind and seeing everything.

WHAT THIS MEANS FOR YOU

I didn't build AYRA just for me. I built it because I've sat across from too many attorneys who remind me of Jim. Too many good people bringing a knife to a gunfight against forces they can't see yet. And the weight of knowing what's coming for them, and watching them operate blind while it approaches, is something I carry every day.

You don't need a $400,000 CMO who can't tell you your cost per case. You don't need a marketing director who has to "check the numbers" and never gets back to you. You need a system that puts the five numbers that determine whether your firm lives or dies in front of your face every single week: cost per case, conversion rate, lead volume by source, revenue per case type, and client acquisition trend. If you can't see those numbers in under five minutes, you're the Titanic. And the iceberg is already out there.

I built AYRA because I had to. Because $2 million disappeared and I swore it would never happen again. Because I'm obsessive and wired to solve problems at 3:00 a.m. in the shower with a Surface Pro.

You don't need to be me. You don't need to disappear into a bathroom for three weeks and build an AI from scratch.

Start tomorrow. Take every process in your firm and record yourself doing it. Loom video. Google Doc. Voice memo. Doesn't matter the format. Break it down so simply that a brand-new hire could execute it on day one without asking you a single question. Build your Toyota factory. Inspect what you expect. And get your five numbers on a dashboard where you can see them every Monday morning. That's the floor. Everything above that is scale.

Or you can wait. The way Jim waited. The way the firm that lost a daughter's catastrophic case waited. The way I waited while $2 million bled out of my company because I trusted the people more than I trusted the data.

The systems will save you. But systems don't build themselves. And they don't run themselves. You need people. The right people in the right seats. People who don't just follow the playbook but rewrite it. People who look at what you've built and make it ten times better.

I spent years learning the difference between the right people and the wrong ones. I paid $2 million in tuition to learn that lesson. And the next hire I made taught me that everything I thought I knew about hiring was wrong.

I didn't look at a resume. I didn't care about past titles or what company he came from. I handed a developer the raw guts of my company and said: "Build me the infrastructure to turn this data into insight."

Forty-eight hours later, he sent me a complete deep wiki. Every data point categorized. Every system mapped. A fully fleshed out architecture for how the information needed to be stored, structured, and called so that nothing would ever hide from me again. I was sitting in my office, fidget spinner in hand, staring at my fifty-seven-inch ultrawide. The way he'd laid everything out. Took a complex problem and boiled it down to the point that I could see the entire business on one screen. That tightness in my chest when you realize someone understood what you were trying to build better than you could have explained it yourself.

The first words out of my mouth were: "This is Developer Jesus."

That developer took AYRA from a prototype in my bathroom to the weapon it is today. And the way I found him will change how you hire forever.

CHAPTER 5

THE RIGHT PEOPLE IN THE RIGHT SEATS

LEFTOVER MEATBALLS. WARMED UP FROM THE MICROWAVE. The smell hit me before I even opened the door, that deep, slow-cooked garlic and tomato that fills a kitchen the way it used to fill my grandmother's. Back when life was simple. Back when the biggest decision I had to make was whether to go outside or watch TV. Before I had a $50 million company. Before I had employees whose mortgages depended on me making the right call. Before I carried the weight of other people's families on my shoulders every single day.

For about ninety seconds, standing at my kitchen counter with a fork in my hand and that smell wrapping around me like a hug from a life I used to live, I wasn't a CEO. I was just a guy eating meatballs. That's all I wanted. To eat a meal while it was still warm.

Then my phone buzzed.

A team member had finished a project I'd assigned. We were migrating every lead in our system to a new platform, rebuilding how we tracked all of our clients. I'd told him exactly what needed to happen. Step by step. Documented. Made it impossible to misunderstand.

I pulled it up on my laptop right there at the counter, fork still in my hand, and felt the blood drain out of my face.

He'd built something that didn't just miss the mark. It broke everything. Leads were routing to the wrong places. Tracking was corrupted. The migration he'd done without double-checking a single step had effectively blown up the system we needed to run the business the next morning. It wasn't a misunderstanding. It was like I'd asked him to rewire a circuit breaker and he'd flooded the basement.

This person had been with me since Fit Pro Syndicate. Years. He'd ridden with me from the gym days through the birth of Case Connect. I trusted him the way you trust someone who's been in the foxhole with you long enough that you stop questioning whether they belong there. When other people on the team complained about him, I made excuses. When his work came back wrong, I fixed it quietly and moved on. I protected him. I felt the weight of his bills, his family, his life depending on this job. Every time I thought about letting him go, I'd tell myself: He's loyal. He's been here from the beginning. I owe him the chance to grow into it.

I kept making that excuse for years. And every year, the excuse cost more.

I stood there looking at the screen. Then I looked at the meatballs. Steam was still rising off them. In about twenty minutes, they wouldn't be.

I walked to my office. Sat down. Spent the next three hours undoing what he'd done and rebuilding it from scratch myself. By the time I came back to the kitchen, the bowl was cold. My wife had already cleaned up. The house was dark. Another evening gone.

I ate those meatballs anyway. Cold, standing in a dark kitchen, because I'm a glutton and because I hadn't eaten since morning. But the pleasure was gone. Every bite was fuel. Survival. Not enjoyment. I stood there chewing and thought about what a perfect metaphor that was for what the wrong hire does to your life. They take the things that are supposed to nourish you, the meals, the evenings, the moments with your family, and they drain every drop of warmth out of them. You still go through the motions. You still eat. You still come home. But you're doing it cold. And the people around you can feel the difference.

A few weeks later, I was in my living room on a Friday afternoon when the email came through. No phone call. No conversation. An email. He was done. No notice. No transition plan. Just a paragraph and a period. I stared at it for about ten seconds. Then I put the phone down, picked it back up, and started calling my team. One by one. Rallying the troops. Redistributing his work. Cleaning up the mess he left behind the same way I'd been cleaning up his messes for years. By the time I went to bed that night, the crisis was contained. Not because it was easy. Because I'd been doing his job alongside mine for so long that absorbing it permanently barely changed my workload.

Then we tried to access the systems that only he controlled. He told us he no longer works here and demanded a consulting fee to hand over the passwords.

That's how I got repaid. For years of protection. For covering for him every time someone on the team told me he wasn't cutting it. And they all told me. Every single one of them. For four years, people I trusted looked me in the eye and said this person was dead weight, and I made excuses because cutting someone loose who'd been in the foxhole with you feels like betrayal. We'd outgrown him four years before that email. I knew it. Everyone knew it. I just couldn't admit that loyalty and capability aren't the same thing.

That's what the wrong hire costs you. Not just money. Time. Energy. The meal you didn't eat. The evening with your kids you didn't have. The slow, grinding realization that you're working harder than you've ever worked and the business isn't moving an inch. You're spinning. Making no progress. Pouring everything you have into managing someone who shouldn't need managing, and by the time you're done cleaning up their mess, you have nothing left. No patience. No presence. No capacity for the things that actually matter.

You come home snippy, wired, and physically in the room but mentally still in your office rebuilding what someone else broke.

Every attorney who's ever managed people knows this feeling. Most of you have accepted it as normal. It's not. It's a symptom of having the wrong people in the chairs.

And it's not just the day-to-day damage. It's the betrayal that comes when you finally find the courage to stop protecting someone and they show you who they really were the entire time. The CMO who ran $1.1 million in untracked spend. The VP who texted his resignation at dawn. The longtime employee who held passwords hostage on his way out. Every one of them had one thing in common: I kept them around too long because firing someone felt like failing them. But keeping them wasn't kindness. It was cowardice dressed up as loyalty. And cowardice always costs more. The best attorney never wins because the best attorney keeps the wrong people in the chairs and calls it loyalty. The best operator fires fast, hires slow, and never confuses comfort with competence.

Chapter 4 ended with a developer who got the raw guts of my company, went dark for 48 hours, and came back with architecture so brilliant the first words out of my mouth were "This is Developer Jesus."

Here's what I didn't tell you. That wasn't just a better hire. That was the moment I stopped believing in resumes, interviews, and credentials forever.

I didn't post a job listing. I didn't screen applicants. A recruiter I trust, a guy who scales and sells businesses, heard my problem and sent me one person. I handed that person a GitHub repository, my Portkey login, and the entire deep wiki of everything I'd built with AYRA. Every Loom video. Every workflow. Every logic tree. The blueprint to my brain, handed to a stranger.

One instruction: Show me what you'd build.

No interview. No "tell me about a time when." No behavioral questions. Just: Here's a real problem. Solve it.

He didn't call me with questions. He didn't ask for clarification. He disappeared into the work the way I disappear into mine. And what came back wasn't an improvement of what I'd given him. He'd taken an engine that worked and turned it into a V12 Lamborghini. Fully finished. Engineered at a level I hadn't even conceptualized. The kind of architecture where you look at it and your chest gets tight because you realize someone understood what you were trying to build better than you could have explained it yourself.

Compare that to the meatball night. Same company. Same type of task. One person takes clear instructions and destroys the system. Another person takes a messy brain dump from a founder at 3:00 a.m. and builds a masterpiece.

The difference isn't intelligence. It's not experience. It's not credentials. It's something you can't find on a resume and can't test in an interview. You can only find it one way.

I CAN'T WORK WITH YOU UNTIL I'VE WORKED WITH YOU

That became the rule. I will not hire anyone, for any role, until I've watched them solve a real problem from inside my company. Not a hypothetical. Not a case study. A living piece of my business, handed to them raw.

A compliance requirement hit California. Twenty attorneys across the state, all with different budgets. Different endpoints for where their leads were routed. Half going to our intake team, half going directly to the firms. New regulation requiring opt-in before any personal information could be collected.

All traffic from every ad platform, every campaign, every source needed to funnel through a single page with a lottery system that paced each attorney's cases dollar-for-dollar against their spend. One page. Twenty clients. Perfect distribution.

I gave a candidate the what. He created the how. Built exactly what we needed. Shipped it. The kind of problem that would've taken a committee three months to scope. He solved it alone.

That's the line between an A-player and everyone else. You give an A-player the destination and they build the road. You give a gopher the destination and they call you from the first intersection asking which way to turn. Then from the second. And the third. And by the time they arrive, you've spent so much time giving directions you could have driven there yourself. Twice.

You find A-players by handing them something real and watching what happens. The ones who come back with questions are gophers. The ones who come back with solutions are keepers. The ones who come back with something better than what you asked for are the people you build a company around.

Resumes won't tell you which one you're looking at. The work will. Every time.

THE SAVAGE

My COO proved it before I ever put him on payroll.

He came through a friend's introduction. But I didn't hire him off the introduction. He started by sending us cases on a CPA deal. Cost per acquisition. He generated leads, ran intake, sent us signed cases. We paid when they converted. Not before.

Think about what that tells you about a person. In an industry full of people who want retainers and guarantees and six-month contracts before they've proven anything, this guy said: Pay me when I produce. He was so confident in what he could deliver that he put his own money on the line before asking for a dollar of mine.

Then he started doing something I never asked him to do.

It was a Slack huddle. His camera was off. Mine was on. Which meant he got to watch my face while he did what he did next.

He pulled up data from our own operation. Our dialer. Our reps. Our numbers. Shared his screen and started pointing at things nobody on my team had caught. This rep right here is burning through leads without converting. This one's numbers look passable, but she's dragging down everyone she works beside. Your dialer is dropping calls during peak hours and nobody's flagged it.

He wasn't showing me problems. He was showing me he'd already diagnosed them. He'd mapped our floor the way a surgeon maps an MRI. And he was sitting there, camera off, watching my jaw come unhinged through my webcam while he calmly told me exactly where to cut.

Then he said something that made me patch Tyler in. "You're losing money here. Here's why. Here's how we're going to fix it. You're about to have the most profitable month of your life."

I watched him work and felt the same thing I'd felt when Developer Jesus sent back the AYRA architecture. That tightness in your chest when you realize: This is different. This person sees what I see. Maybe more.

Bad hires create fires and throw them at your feet. A-players find smoke before it becomes a fire, put it out, and fix the root cause. Then they send you a message: "This happened. I noticed this. I did that. Should be good in a few days. Will keep you updated."

That message is the most beautiful set of sentences a founder or a managing partner will ever read. It means someone else is watching. Someone else is losing sleep over the details so you don't have to.

Here's how you find these people.

Stop interviewing. Start testing. Take the hardest problem sitting on your desk right now. The one you've been putting off. The intake process that needs rebuilding. The billing system that leaks revenue. The marketing report nobody can figure out how to pull. Whatever it is, strip it down to a clear problem statement: here's what's broken, here's what success looks like, here's access to the data.

Hand it to a candidate. Give them 48 hours. Then shut up and watch.

The ones who call you with questions before they've tried anything are gophers. They need directions at every intersection. The ones who come back with a workable solution are keepers. The ones who come back with something better than what you asked for, something you hadn't even considered, are the people you build a company around. That's how I found Developer Jesus. That's how I found the engineer who built our California compliance system in days. That's how I found my COO. None of them impressed me in a conversation. They impressed me with their work.

The résumé tells you where someone has been. The microproject tells you what they can do right now, inside your business, with your problems. One of those predicts success. The other predicts a good interview.

MARGATE

My wife drove. She always drove. For as long as I'd run Case Connect, I'd been the guy in the passenger seat of our Escalade with a laptop balanced on my thighs, trying not to throw up. I get carsick. Always have. Staring at a screen while a 5,700-pound SUV hurtles down the expressway is my personal version of hell. But the alternative was not watching the dashboard, and not watching the dashboard meant another $800,000-loss month. So I sat there, green in the face, one hand on the keyboard and the other gripping the door handle as my wife commandeered her lane and whatever adjacent lane she felt like borrowing. Three kids in the back. A woman who drives like she's being pursued by the law in the front. And me in between, trying to read a P&L at eighty miles per hour without redecorating the windshield with my lunch.

That was every car ride. Every trip to the shore. Every Saturday. I couldn't be present because being present meant closing the laptop, and closing the laptop meant not catching the campaign that was bleeding $3,000 a day. So I white-knuckled it through the nausea and kept scrolling. Even when my girls were building sandcastles three feet in front of me, half of me was somewhere else. Checking. Bracing. Waiting for whatever broke next.

My wife would glance over at me. She never said it. She didn't have to. The look said: You're here but you're not here. And she was right. I was never fully anywhere.

Then we went to Margate. Same shore town where the attorney once stood up in a restaurant and told strangers I was famous while my daughter ate a crayon.

This time, I left the laptop in the car. I made it about ten steps before my hand twitched. I turned around. Walked back to the Escalade. Reached for the door handle. The car didn't sense the key fob. My wife had it in her bag, already halfway to the beach with the girls. I stood there with my hand on the handle of a locked car, staring at the laptop through the tinted glass, and something in my chest unclenched. Maybe it was fate. Maybe it was just a dead battery in a key fob. But that little bit of resistance was enough. I'll grab it later if I need it. I didn't need it.

Will Smith once described what it feels like to jump out of an airplane. You worry about the plane. You worry about the chute. You worry about everything that could go wrong. And then you're standing at the open door, and the panic hits maximum. You don't want to go. Every cell in your body screams, "Don't do this!" Then you jump. And the second you're in the air, the fear disappears. You realize this is the most beautiful thing you've ever experienced. Everything you were afraid of dissolves, and the only thing left is the feeling of being fully, completely alive.

That's what it felt like leaving the laptop behind. My CTO and COO told me they had it handled. And for the first time in years, I believed them. Not because they said the words.

Because they'd proven it, over and over, in ways that couldn't be faked. The jump wasn't blind faith. It was earned trust. I walked onto the sand with nothing in my hands. The salt air hit my skin and I felt the sun on my arms and I realized I couldn't remember the last time I'd gone to the beach without a screen between me and my kids.

That night, everyone was asleep.

I was sitting at the table in our morning room. The house smelled like sunscreen and salt. I opened my phone expecting damage control.

What I was looking at was the best day in the history of the company.

Record numbers. The dashboard of the call center was glowing on my screen. Matt, our COO, was texting me. He said he'd been refreshing every second and couldn't put his phone down. The CTO had spotted a campaign issue that morning, diagnosed it, and fixed it before it cost us a dollar. Matt had pulled rep performance data, restructured the floor, and improved conversion rates by the afternoon. They'd found each other's blind spots. Communicated without me in the middle. Made decisions I would have made, and in some cases, better ones.

I couldn't sit still. I ran upstairs. My wife was in bed, half-asleep, and I was standing in the doorway rattling off every new sign-up like a kid reading a Christmas list. "Another one just came in. And another. You're not going to believe this." She laughed. She didn't understand the dashboard. She didn't need to. She understood me. And she could see it on my face: Something had changed.

The system was running. The numbers were better without me in the room. Not because I wasn't needed. Because the people I'd put in place were A-players who didn't need me hovering to perform. They needed the what. They built the how.

That's the feeling you're chasing. Whether you know it or not. Every attorney grinding eighteen-hour days, every managing partner who can't take a week off without the firm collapsing, every solo practitioner who *is* the firm. You're not chasing more cases. You're not chasing more revenue. You're chasing the moment where you check your phone expecting wreckage and find a record day instead.

We exported our COO's brain into AYRA. Every pattern he catches, every instinct he's built from years of running high-volume operations, we trained the AI to think exactly how he does. The system delivers his insights in real time, faster than any human could.

But the AI didn't replace him. It multiplied him. A-players and great systems don't compete. They compound. The person makes the system smarter. The system makes the person faster. And the founder gets to eat his meatballs while they're still warm.

THE CALL FROM TURKS

My phone rang on a Tuesday afternoon. Tyler's name on the screen.

I picked up expecting business. A question about spend. A client issue. Something operational. That's what Tuesday afternoon calls were.

Instead, I heard waves.

"Bro," Tyler said. "I'm sitting on a beach in Turks and Caicos right now. The kids are in the water. My wife is reading a book. I haven't opened my laptop in four days. And you know what happened at the firm today?"

I waited.

"Nothing. Nothing happened. Because nothing needed

to happen. The team ran it. Cases signed. Clients managed. Demands went out. Nobody called me. Nobody needed me. The machine just ran."

I could hear his kids screaming in the background. The happy kind. The kind of screaming that means someone just got knocked over by a wave and thought it was the funniest thing in the world.

Tyler Wilk. Maxed-out credit card. GOT WILK? ad that bombed. Zero clients. The guy I almost failed. Now sitting on a chartered jet's worth of beach, watching his kids play in water that costs more per night than his first month of ad spend, while his law firm printed money without him touching a single thing.

He didn't get there by accident. He used the same recruiter. Tested people before he hired them. Invested in talent that cost real money. Built the systems from this book and then staffed them with people who didn't just follow the playbook but rewrote it.

"You know what the crazy part is?" Tyler said. "I used to think nobody could run it like me. Turns out the right people run it different. And different is better."

I hung up and sat there for a minute. Because that's the whole book in one sentence. The best attorney never wins because the best attorney tries to do everything. The one who builds the machine, hires the people, and gets out of the way? That's the one on the beach.

You've got the system. You've got the playbook. You've got the framework for hiring people who'll run it without you. But none of it matters if you don't ask yourself the question most attorneys never ask.

What is your firm actually worth?

Not what you think it's worth. Not what you hope it's worth.

What would someone write a check for, today, to own what you've built? And what could that number be if you stopped running a practice and started building a company?

That number might be the difference between working until you die and walking away with generational wealth. And the gap between where you are and where you could be is smaller than you think. If you know where to look.

CHAPTER 6

LAWYER TO CEO (THE ENDGAME)

I WAS IN MY UPSTAIRS OFFICE WHEN THE CALL CAME. LATE afternoon. The sun was low enough that light cut through the window at an angle, the kind that turns every particle of dust into something you can see. Little specks drifting through the beam like they had nowhere to be and all the time in the world to get there. I watched them for a second before picking up.

It was about a firm we worked with. Good firm. Serious operation. They'd sent us new retainers out of nowhere a few weeks earlier. Updated agreements. Different terms. My team noticed it before I did. Something felt off.

So I called someone at the firm. Asked what was going on.

The person on the other end smirked. I could hear it through the phone. "I can't disclose that."

I heard through the grapevine a few days later. The firm had sold. Nine figures. Not mid-eight. Not "approaching nine." Nine figures. A personal injury law firm, in this market, walked away with a number that most attorneys wouldn't believe if you showed it to them on a napkin.

"No fucking way," I said it out loud. To nobody. In an empty office. Then I called back and made them repeat it.

I stood up from my desk and walked back to the window. Those dust particles were still floating through the beam. Same office. Same Tuesday afternoon. But the number had changed the air in the room. Because I knew something the rest of the industry didn't yet. We'd helped build that machine. Our marketing. Our leads. Our system feeding their pipeline for years. And that pipeline, combined with everything else they'd built, was worth nine figures to a buyer who understood what they were looking at.

That's not a law firm. That's a company. And the difference between the two is what this chapter is about.

THE PHONE CALL IN THE BATHROOM

You met Joey in the Introduction. Kitchen island. Stool. MacBook Pro. Sleeping baby on my chest. That was Case Connect's headquarters. A $50 million company in its underwear.

Joey signed on. Spent $1,600 his first month. Signed 7 or 8 cases. Called me and said: "Is this a scam?"

It wasn't. He kept going. Tripled down. Hired the right people. Built systems. Treated every client like family. And in two years, Joey went from a few hundred grand a year to a mid-eight-figure exit.

When he called me to tell me the deal was done, I was sitting on the edge of the bathtub in my daughters' bathroom. Around 7:15 at night. Both girls in the tub. The faucet was running, that steady white-noise drone that fills a small bathroom until it becomes the air itself. My youngest was splashing. My oldest was pressing foam letters onto the tile wall, building a word she'd probably forget by morning.

Joey's voice cut through the humidity.

He told me it was done. The number. The terms. All of it. His words were steady but there was something underneath them. The sound of a man who still couldn't believe the sentence coming out of his own mouth.

I cocked my head to the side. Stood up from the edge of the tub and stepped into the hallway so I could hear him better, pulling the door half-closed behind me. The faucet noise faded. Joey's voice got clearer. And standing there in the hallway between my daughters' bath time and the biggest phone call of my career, I felt something I didn't expect.

Pride. Not for me. For him. For what we'd built together from a kitchen island and sixteen hundred dollars. And underneath the pride, a sadness I wasn't ready for. Joey wasn't just a client. He was the guy who called me about everything. Business. Life. Decisions that had nothing to do with cases. Now a different firm would take over the account. That chapter was closing. You don't realize how much a relationship means to you until the reason for it changes.

I told him I was proud of him. Went back into the bathroom. My daughter dropped a foam letter in the water, and it made that soft plop sound that somehow made the whole moment feel more real than any boardroom handshake ever could.

Later that night, after the girls were asleep, I was talking to my wife about it. And it hit me. I had a huge impact on that. I helped generate wealth for someone. I helped change a man's life, his family's life, his future. From a sleeping baby on my chest and a sixteen-hundred-dollar ad spend to a number most people can't fathom. That realization sat in my chest like a warm stone.

Joey went from living with his parents to living in a multi-million-dollar house. Got a new G63. Got engaged. Everything he'd been grinding for materialized in two years because he did the one thing most attorneys refuse to do. He treated his firm like a business, not a practice.

And here's what separates Joey from every attorney who plateaus. He's back. Right now. In the legal space again. Lemon law. Other verticals. Building the same machine in a different category, except this time he's doing it with every lesson from round one already loaded. He's not hoping for an exit. He's engineering one from day one. His first month in lemon law, the cost per case came back at $683. Six hundred and eighty-three dollars. That number hit me like the beginning of 2020 all over again, when MVA costs were so low they felt like a misprint. Same playbook. Different vertical. Same results.

Joey marketed relentlessly. He was paranoid when new cases stopped coming in. He couldn't sleep if the machine wasn't fed. That 24/7 obsession, that inability to coast, that refusal to take his foot off the gas even when the numbers looked good. That's not a personality flaw. That's the engine behind every eight-figure exit in this industry.

THE UNICORN

Nick and Steve had tried everything before they found us. Every lead gen company known to man. Every pitch. Every promise. Years of searching for something that actually worked. They'd been burned so many times that the word "marketing" probably tasted like ash in their mouths by the time someone mentioned Case Connect.

Their first month with us, they spent $25,000. Today they spend over $600,000. Every month. That's not a typo. Six hundred thousand dollars a month. Because when you find something that prints money, you don't tap the brakes. You weld the gas pedal to the floor.

I want to tell you about a call with Nick that taught me more about why he wins than any data point ever could.

His firm had just come off record days. Numbers that would make most attorneys retire on the spot. Then one day dipped. Just one. Slightly below average. Not a disaster. Not a crisis. A blip.

Nick called me. His voice started the way it always does, words tumbling fast like he's trying to outrun the thought forming behind them. "I hope we're okay. Do you think things will bounce back? We really can't lose traction right now, we're at a pivotal point in the month." Then it downshifted. The words slowed and softened into something close to a whisper, each one landing with a kind of quiet weight that floated through the phone and settled in your chest. That's how Nick talks when something matters. He starts at full speed and then the intensity compresses until every syllable carries more than the last.

One mediocre day. After records. And his response was to call me like the building was on fire.

That's the wiring. That refusal to accept a single day of average. Most attorneys would look at a dip after a record stretch and tell themselves it's normal. Nick looked at it like a threat that needed to be eliminated before it spread. He doesn't accept "it is what it is." He tears things apart and rebuilds them until the result matches the picture in his head. It's a kind of productive delusion. Stressful as hell to live with. But it's the reason his firm files on almost all of their cases, his settlements are better than most firms I've worked with, and his clients don't leave.

My business partner once put a fake lead into Nick's system. Just to test the backend. See how his team handled it. He told me later that they called the number so many times he had to block it. And here's the part that still gets me. Nick's team runs on a manual dialer. Not an auto-dialer. Not the kind of power dialer we use with 1,500 seats. Manual. A rep pressing call on a single lead twenty times in one day. At a scale where I wouldn't recommend it, his people are so relentless, so trained, so infected by Nick's standard that they turn a manual system into a machine through sheer force of will.

That's what a real operation looks like. Not the technology. The people. People who've absorbed the founder's refusal to lose and made it their own.

We've grown together over the years. A lot of our clients become family that way. It's not a sales pitch. It's what happens when you fight in the trenches with someone long enough. You stop being vendor and client and start being people who built something together. When we found out we were having our most recent daughter, Angelia, there was a Hermès baby blanket and matching Burberry outfits for all three girls waiting at my house before we'd even told most people. I ran to my wife and showed her. She held up the blanket and the little outfits, and neither of us said anything for a second. That's who Nick is. He shows up.

Nick will sell his firm one day. And when he does, the number will probably make a few of the attorneys reading this faint. Because he didn't just build a law firm. He built a machine that a buyer would kill to own. One that prints cases, retains clients, and runs whether Nick is in the office or on a beach somewhere not answering his phone.

That's the difference between a practice and a company. And it's the difference between retiring comfortably and generational wealth.

Every attorney I've ever worked with knows, intellectually, that they need to stop doing everything. They've heard it at conferences. They've read it in books. They've nodded along at masterminds and then gone right back to grinding eighteen-hour days because knowing isn't doing. Never has been.

The hardest part isn't learning new skills. It's letting go of old ones. You went to law school. You spent years becoming a great attorney. You wear that identity like armor. And now someone is telling you the path to wealth requires you to stop doing the thing you trained for and start doing the thing nobody ever taught you.

That's the pill most attorneys can't swallow.

Remember Tyler in Chapter 5? On a beach in Turks and Caicos. Kids in the water. Wife reading a book. Hadn't opened his laptop in four days. Before that call, Tyler's life looked like every attorney reading this book. On and off meetings. Answering calls in the middle of other calls. Juggling thirty things at once with three little kids at home. He was the firm. Without him in the chair, nothing moved.

The shift happened when he stopped being the one in the chair and started being the one who chose who sat in it. He hired A-players. Tested them before they got the job. Invested in talent that cost real money. And one Tuesday afternoon, the machine ran a perfect day without him touching a single thing.

I have a writing desk in the middle of my office. Light oak. A "Chasing Dreams" Lamborghini Revuelto calendar on it with Mont Blanc fountain pens and special ink next to them. Bookshelves along the walls filled with every business and marketing book I've read in the last decade. Model supercars on the shelves, little replicas of cars I've bought over the years.

I was pacing circles around that desk on a Monday morning.

Not because anything was wrong. Because that's what I do. I pace. I scan. I'm always waiting for the thing that's about to break. That's been my operating system for years. The heavy feeling on your chest that something is lurking around the corner. The unprompted Slack huddle. The message just sitting there waiting to grab you and pull you into its world of horror.

I stopped in front of the bookshelf. Glanced at one of the model cars. Checked my phone.

Nothing.

No fires. No emergencies. No one needed me to fix what someone else broke. The COO had it. The CTO had it. The team was running and nobody had called. I stood there for a second, phone in hand, and realized I'd been pacing out of habit, not necessity. The dread was gone. Not suppressed. Not buried under work. Gone. Like fog that burns off so slowly you don't notice it lifting until suddenly you can see the whole road in front of you.

That feeling doesn't arrive all at once. It builds. One quiet Monday becomes two. Then a week. Then you stop bracing every time your phone buzzes. And you start to understand that this is what it was supposed to feel like all along.

THE NUMBER THAT CHANGES EVERYTHING

I was on a call with an attorney a few months back. Good firm. Real results. Netting around $2 million a year. He asked me what I thought his firm was worth.

I was pacing around that same desk. Slow circles. One hand on the phone, the other trailing along the edge of the oak. I do this when I'm about to tell someone something they don't want to hear. I pace like I'm winding up.

"Walk me through the operation," I said. "Who runs marketing?"

"I do."

"Who manages intake?"

"I oversee it."

"Who handles the business development?"

"That's me."

"And if you leave for a month, what happens?"

I stopped pacing. Because his silence told me everything. The kind of silence where you can hear someone recalculating the value of their entire career.

Here's what I told him. Nobody is buying a name anymore. They're buying a system. A flywheel. An engine that can be fed and scaled. If you're doing $2 million in EBITDA and you *are* the marketer, the intake manager, the COO, and the CEO, a buyer will subtract the cost of replacing all four of those roles from your number. Every hat you wear becomes a deduction. Then they'll make you stay on for two years after the sale to make sure the transition doesn't collapse.

You thought you were selling for $6 million. After adjustments, you're looking at $3 million and a two-year earn-out where you're still doing everything you were doing before, except now someone else owns the company.

That's the reality of selling a practice. The best attorney built something worth his time. The best operator built something worth someone else's money. Same decade of work. Different zeros on the check.

Now here's the reality of selling a company.

Get your EBITDA above $5 million. Diversify into multiple verticals. Build the machine so it runs without you. Document every system. Train a team that doesn't need the founder in the building. When your net hits $8 million across three verticals with a proven acquisition engine and a management team that operates independently, you're not getting a 4x multiple. You're getting 8x. Maybe 10x. Maybe more.

So, $8 million at 10x is an $80 million company. That's not retirement money. That's dynasty money. The kind where your grandchildren's grandchildren never worry about it.

And the proof is on the table. Joey took a $1,600 ad spend and turned it into a mid-eight-figure exit. When the same playbook hit lemon law at $683 a case, the system didn't care that the vertical was different. It cared that the fundamentals were right. What works in MVA, when it's dialed in, works everywhere. Mass tort. Workers' comp. Lemon law. A lead comes in. A human answers the phone. They connect with someone in pain. They build trust. They close. The only thing that changes is the case type and the team that works it on the legal side. Copy the machine. Paste it into the new vertical. Scale.

The catch is those first three words. When it's dialed in. If your intake doesn't convert, if your marketing bleeds cash, if you're the attorney with $400,000 in payroll who can't tell me your cost per case, expanding into another vertical won't save you. It'll bankrupt you faster. But if the machine is built? Expanding is like flipping a light switch in a new room. The electricity is already running through the walls. You just need to screw in the bulb.

That nine-figure exit I told you about at the top of this chapter? That firm had the machine. Multi-vertical. Systems documented. Team in place. Growth trajectory that made a buyer salivate. They weren't selling a law firm. They were selling a company. And the buyer paid a company price.

I was sitting in the car outside Target. My wife was inside. The kids were napping in the back seat, that particular silence where you can hear them breathing and you don't dare move because if one of them wakes up, the other follows, and then Target becomes a hostage negotiation.

My phone buzzed. Another PDF from my buddy. The guy I used to work with on the dealership floor. Same showroom. Same opportunities. Same customer base. Same hours. The only difference was what we did with them.

This time it was vending machines. He'd put together a whole plan. Locations. Revenue projections. Vendor contacts. The kind of document that looks like progress but isn't, because no vending machine was ever going to get plugged in. I knew it before I opened the attachment. The same way I knew the YouTube channel wasn't going to happen. The same way I knew the last three ideas before this one were dead on arrival.

I listened. Asked him a few questions. Not hard ones. Just enough to make him think through the gaps. How much upfront capital? Who maintains them? What's the margin after location fees? Gentle questions. The kind a friend asks when he doesn't want to say what he's actually thinking.

He started defending it. Not answering the questions. Defending the idea against them. And that's when I knew. He didn't call me for input. He called me for validation. His mind was already made up. He just needed someone to tell him it was brilliant so the dopamine would hit and he could ride it for another few weeks before the next thing caught his eye.

I never heard about the vending machines again.

That's what I call an askhole. Always asking. Never acting. He watched where people made money. He studied it. He talked about it until talking about it started to feel like doing it. And then he moved on to the next thing that would get the same treatment.

I'm not telling you this to be cruel. I'm telling you because right now, at this exact moment, you're at a fork. You can close this chapter and say "that was interesting" and go back to doing exactly what you were doing yesterday. Or you can do something about what you just read.

The difference between the attorneys who build eight-figure firms and the ones who grind until they burn out isn't intelligence. It isn't luck. It isn't some connection or secret handshake. It's execution. The willingness to take what you've learned and act on it before the motivation fades. Before the excuses show up. Before "let me think about it" becomes the theme song of your career.

Jim thought about it. Joey executed. One closed his practice. The other sold for mid-eight-figures. Same industry. Same opportunity. One variable.

You already know what that variable is.

THE THING THAT WOKE ME UP AT NIGHT

I want to leave you with something that's going to change the temperature of this book.

Everything I've shown you in this chapter is real. The exits. The multiples. The math. The possibility of building something worth more than you've ever imagined. All of it is on the table for any attorney willing to do the work.

But there's something I haven't told you yet. Something I've been holding back because I needed you to see the opportunity before I showed you the threat.

I used to feel like I was playing in the NBA while most PI attorneys were playing JV ball. Not because I'm smarter.

Because I understood marketing and acquisition at a level that the legal industry hadn't seen. The competition wasn't competition. It was target practice.

That feeling is gone.

There are people coming into this industry right now who make me nervous. Not course grifters. Not small-time marketers with stolen ad templates. Real operators. People who've sold companies, taken them public, bought them back, and done it again. People from solar and Medicare and insurance. Industries where the margins are thinner, the competition is meaner, and the operators are hungrier than anything the legal world has ever produced.

Some of them tried to buy Case Connect. Not to partner with us. To plug our system into their own machine and run it without us. I felt it in my gut when those calls started coming in. The way you feel a storm before the sky changes color. The air gets heavy. The birds go quiet. And you know something is about to hit that you can't stop.

I don't want to just be a good player anymore. I want to be Kobe. Because when NBA-level operators start flooding the court, the JV players don't just lose. They get carried off on stretchers. And right now, most PI attorneys don't even know the game has changed.

I know exactly who these people are. I've sat across from them. I've watched them build. I've seen what they do to industries that thought they were safe.

And I'm going to tell you everything. What they're doing. How they're doing it. And exactly how much time you have left before the door closes for good.

CHAPTER 7

THE SHARKS ARE COMING

I WAS ON FACETIME WITH A GUY I'D BEEN DOING BUSINESS with when he flipped the camera.

"Watch this," he said.

The screen swung away from his face and I was looking at a room. A massive, open room in Boca Raton, Florida. Two hundred seats. Every one of them filled. The sound hit me first, even through the tiny speaker on my phone. Keyboards clacking like a rainstorm on a tin roof. Voices layered on top of voices, not yelling but pushing, the sound of two hundred people leaning into their headsets and driving conversations forward with an energy that made the air in the room feel carbonated. Everyone was dressed casual. T-shirts. Hoodies. The uniform of people who don't need to look important because the scoreboard on the wall does that for them. I could feel the heat through the screen. Not temperature. Intensity. The kind of room where the air itself has a pulse.

These people weren't attorneys. They weren't paralegals. They weren't legal marketers. They were operators from solar, ACA, and Medicare. Industries where you have to convince a healthy person to spend money they don't want to spend on a product they're not sure they need. That's an NBA-level sales environment. You either close or you starve. There is no referral network. There is no reputation to fall back on. Every dollar is earned on the phone, in real time, against a hundred competitors doing the same thing.

And they were looking at personal injury the way a lion looks at a limping gazelle.

The guy flipped the camera back to his face. He wasn't smiling. He was calm. The kind of calm that comes from knowing something the rest of the world hasn't figured out yet.

I told you what he said back in Chapter 1. "You're selling free money." Four words. When you first read them, you didn't know what they meant. Not really. You hadn't sat through Maria's intake call yet. You hadn't watched $100,000 turn into 5 signed cases and then 57. You hadn't seen what a $2 million loss looks like on a screen at eye level, or what happens when a developer turns a founder's 3:00 a.m. brain dump into a weapon.

Now you know. And those four words should land in your chest like a cinder block.

Because he wasn't wrong. To operators who've spent their careers in solar and Medicare, industries where you have to convince a healthy person to part with money they don't want to spend, personal injury looks like the easiest sale on earth. The client is already hurt. They already need a lawyer. And the people standing between them and the money? He looked right through the camera and said it the way a surgeon describes a routine procedure. No malice. Just certainty.

Sometimes you get comfortable. You stop measuring the threat because the threat has been theoretical for so long it starts to feel like a rumor. That call ended the rumor. I sat there holding my phone and felt the same thing a boxer feels when he watches tape of his next opponent for the first time and realizes this one is different. This one isn't here to compete. This one is here to end you.

WHAT THEY DO WHEN THEY GET INSIDE

Let me tell you what happens when private equity acquires a personal injury firm. Not in theory. In practice. In the lives of real people.

The first thing they do is audit everything. Every case. Every employee. Every dollar in and out. They're not looking for what's working. They're looking for what's inefficient. And in most PI firms, inefficiency is everywhere, because the firm was built by a lawyer who cared about clients, not by an operator who cares about margins.

Then the cuts start.

You know that case manager who's been with the firm for fifteen years? The one who knows every client by name? The one who stays late because Mrs. Rodriguez needs help understanding her settlement documents and nobody else has the patience? The woman who raised her kids on that salary and doesn't have enough in retirement savings to walk away even if she wanted to? She's gone. Her salary is a line item. Her institutional knowledge is invisible to a spreadsheet. Her replacement is a system, a process, an automated workflow that costs a fraction of what she did and processes cases three times faster.

The paralegal who's been there since the firm opened? The one who brought a casserole to the attorney's house when his wife had surgery? Gone. The receptionist who remembers every client's name when they walk through the door? Gone. Replaced by a voice-bot that routes calls faster than any human can.

The injured clients become inventory. Cases get churned

through a machine designed to maximize return on investment, not to maximize the outcome for the human being on the other end. Quick settlements. Volume over value. The goal isn't to fight for the best result. The goal is to close the file and move to the next one. The grandmother who slipped in a grocery store and can't walk without a cane? She's a number now. Her case gets settled for whatever clears the pipeline fastest, not whatever makes her whole. The family who lost someone in a wreck? Their grief has a dollar sign next to it and a target resolution date that has nothing to do with justice and everything to do with quarterly earnings.

This isn't speculation. It already happened in solar. It already happened in Medicare. The same playbook, the same operators, the same financial engineering. And the attorneys who sold their firms? Some of them are stuck in two-year earnouts, watching everything they built get dismantled by people who see their life's work as an asset to be optimized. Walking into their own office every morning and not recognizing it. Sitting in meetings where the conversation is about throughput and case velocity instead of clients and outcomes.

And here's the part that should make your skin crawl. They're more efficient. They *are* more effective at extracting profit from the machine. That's why they win. Not because they're better for clients. Because they're better at making money. And in a world where the best attorney never wins, the best operator always does.

WHAT IT LOOKS LIKE IN YOUR MARKET

Let me paint you a picture.

You're running your firm. You've been doing this for a decade. You know your market. You know the judges. You know the insurance adjusters by first name. You've built something real, on your own, case by case, referral by referral.

One morning you open Google and search "car accident lawyer" in your city. And there's a name you've never seen before. Sitting above your listing. Above everyone's listing. Running ads with production quality that looks like a Super Bowl commercial. A website so clean and so fast it makes yours look like it was built in 2008. Reviews flooding in. Five stars. Hundreds of them.

You click around. You realize this firm didn't exist six months ago. They opened an office in your city, hired three associate attorneys at salary, plugged into a call center that handles intake 24 hours a day, deployed an ad budget that dwarfs your annual revenue, and started vacuuming every case in your zip code before you finished your morning coffee.

They didn't earn their way into your market. They bought their way in. And they'll outspend you every single day until you're the one picking up the phone and it's not ringing.

That's not a hypothetical. That's what's happening right now in markets across the country. The PE-backed firms don't grow the way you grew. They deploy. Like a military operation. City by city. State by state. And by the time you realize they're in your market, they've been there for months.

THE SECOND WAVE

Private equity is the first wave. The second wave is quieter and potentially more dangerous.

Alternative Business Structures. ABS. The legal framework that allows non-lawyers to own and operate law firms. Arizona was the first state to open the door. A guy I know, runs a nationwide firm, grew up near me. He already has one in Arizona. They're all doing it. Marketers, operators, tech companies. People who used to sell leads to attorneys are now cutting out the middleman entirely. They're running cases through an ABS, hiring attorneys as employees instead of partners, and keeping the margin that used to belong to the firm.

Think about what that means. The people who used to need you no longer need you. The marketing companies, the lead generators, the tech platforms. They can own the client relationship from first click to final settlement. The attorney becomes a commodity. A licensee. A cog in someone else's machine. The same thing I was at the Mercedes dealership before I figured out how to build my own.

Arizona is the crack in the dam. Other states are watching. When the revenue numbers come in, and they will, because operators who understand acquisition will print money in this model, more states will follow. The question isn't if this spreads. It's when. And by the time it reaches your state, the firms that prepared for it will be the ones still standing. The ones that didn't will be working for the people who saw it coming.

THE MATH THAT SHOULD TERRIFY YOU

There are 48,000 personal injury firms in this country. You've read that number before in this book. I need you to read it one more time and sit with what it actually means.

My gut tells me 40 percent of them will be gone within the next decade. Not merged. Not acquired. Gone. Doors closed. Names removed from buildings. The attorney who spent twenty years building a practice will be working for someone else, the way Jim is right now. Assuming he's still practicing at all.

That number isn't based on a spreadsheet. It's based on watching what happened to every other industry when well-funded operators showed up with better systems, more capital, and zero sentimentality about how things used to be done. Taxi drivers thought Uber was a fad. Bookstore owners thought Amazon was a website. Hotel chains thought Airbnb was a joke. Every single one of them said the same thing: "Our industry is different. That can't happen here."

It's happening here. Right now. While you're reading this.

The operators I watched through that FaceTime screen in Boca Raton aren't coming. They're already here. They're already buying firms. Already deploying tech stacks that cost more per month than most PI firms make in a year. Already building call centers that make the one I showed you look like a lemonade stand. And they have one advantage that no amount of legal talent can overcome: They understand acquisition. They understand systems. They understand scale. And they are pathologically, genetically incapable of accepting inefficiency.

Your law degree won't save you. Your twenty years of experience won't save you. Your reputation in the community won't save you. The twenty-two-year veteran I told you about in Chapter 1, the one whose phone stopped ringing? He had all of those things. He's gone.

THE TWO ATTORNEYS

Close your eyes for a second. I want to show you something.

Picture two attorneys. Same city. Same practice area. Same talent. Same case volume today. Both reading this book at the same time. Same page. Same sentence.

One of them closes this book and says "that was interesting" and goes back to doing exactly what he was doing yesterday. The askhole from the Target parking lot, except with a law degree. He'll think about it. He'll mention it to his partner. He'll put it on a list of things to do after the trial next month. And the trial after that. And the one after that. "Let me think about it" becomes the background music of his career until one day the music stops and there's nothing left to think about.

The other attorney does something different. She reads this chapter, and her stomach drops. Not from fear. From recognition. She's seen the signs. The phones ringing less. The cases getting harder to sign. The new firms showing up in her market with budgets that dwarf hers. She's felt the ground shifting, and now she understands why.

Tomorrow morning, she pulls up her intake data. Actually looks at it. The real numbers, not the ones her team tells her. She finds out she's converting at 7 percent. She does the math from Chapter 3 and watches $1.6 million a year in lost revenue materialize on her screen like a ghost that's been standing in the room the whole time. She sits there the way that attorney sat on the Zoom when I typed the numbers into the calculator. Ten seconds of nothing. "That can't be right."

It's right. And it's been right every month for the last three years.

She calls her office manager. "We're changing how we answer the phone. Starting today." She trains her team the way Chris handled Maria. Not as a checklist. As a conversation. Find the nerve. Widen the gap. Set the wall. She fires two reps who've been answering calls like they're working the DMV and replaces them with hungry, trainable people who actually care about the voice on the other end of the line.

She pulls up a Loom and records her billing process at midnight, whispering into the microphone the way I did in my kitchen with no shirt on, because the people in her house are sleeping and the people in her firm need a system they can follow without calling her every ten minutes.

She starts measuring cost per case. Not cost per lead. The real number. She stops hiring off resumes and starts handing candidates real problems, then watches what happens in 48 hours. She finds her Developer Jesus. Her COO who pulls up data nobody else caught on a Slack huddle with his camera off, and says: "You're about to have the most profitable month of your life."

She builds the machine. Not because she read a book about it. Because she *felt* what the people in this book felt. She felt Sandy's terror in that wobbling chair under fluorescent lights with bass thumping through the walls. She felt Maria's relief when Chris asked "What does that feel like for you specifically?" and the walls came down. She felt the silence of the attorney on that Zoom, watching $1.6 million in losses appear on a calculator. She felt the weight of Jim's "thank you" on his front porch, and she swore she'd never be the one saying it.

Three years later, her firm runs without her in the building. Her intake converts at 35 percent. Her cost per case is half what it was. She expanded into a second vertical the way Joey did with lemon law at $683 a case, because the machine didn't care what case type it processed. It cared that the fundamentals were right. Her COO handles the floor. Her systems document themselves. She checks her phone on a Tuesday afternoon, expecting damage control, and finds a record day. The same feeling I had sitting at a table in Margate, smelling sunscreen and salt and staring at a dashboard that glowed.

A buyer offered her 8x. She told them to come back when the number started with a different digit.

She went to the beach last Saturday. Left her laptop in the car. Her daughter built a sandcastle, and she watched the whole thing.

The other attorney? His firm closed eighteen months ago.

He's working at someone else's practice now. A PE-backed operation where the cases move through a pipeline and the clients are inventory, and the woman who used to manage his files got replaced by software. He sits in a cubicle that used to be a corner office and wonders what went wrong. He tells himself the market changed. Tells himself marketing doesn't work. Tells himself the same story Jim told himself on that front porch while the camera was too close and the street was too quiet and there was no office left to call from.

Same book. Same information. Same opportunity. One variable.

It was always one variable.

WHAT I'M ASKING YOU TO DO

I built Case Connect because nobody else was building what attorneys needed. I built AYRA because I sat across from too many attorneys who reminded me of Jim, and I couldn't carry that weight without doing something about it. I wrote this book because the system works and the clock is ticking and the people reading these words deserve to know both of those things before the window closes.

Every chapter gave you something real. A way to find clients that actually works. A way to close them that turns strangers into family. A system for building infrastructure that doesn't collapse the second you leave the room. A method for finding people who make the machine better instead of breaking it. A blueprint for turning a practice into a company worth more than you ever imagined.

Not one piece of it requires you to work with me. Not one chapter was written so you'd pick up the phone and call Case Connect. I gave you the playbook. The whole thing. The same playbook that took Tyler from a maxed-out credit card to a Rolls Royce Spectre with mandarin interior pulling into my driveway while my daughters pressed their faces against the window. The same playbook that took Joey from a kitchen island pitch with a sleeping baby to a mid-eight-figure exit in two years. The same playbook that took Nick from $25,000 a month to $600,000 a month because he refused to accept a single day of average.

The sharks are in the water. I can see them from where I'm standing. I've sat across from them. I've watched them circle. I know what they do to industries that thought they were safe.

You can build the machine yourself. Every tool is in your hands. Or you can partner with someone who's already built it, who's spent $200 million learning what works and what doesn't, who has the call center and the AI and the infrastructure and the obsession to keep improving it every single day.

Either way, do something. Do it now. Not next quarter. Not after the next trial. Not after you "think about it."

Because Jim thought about it. And the last time I saw him, he was on a porch that wasn't his, with a camera too close to his face, thanking me for telling him no.

Don't be Jim.

EPILOGUE

MY OLDEST DAUGHTER WAS STANDING IN THE MIDDLE OF the kitchen. It was after dinner. The plates were still on the counter. The house had that post-meal haze where everyone is full and loose, and nobody wants to move.

She started doing something. At first I didn't understand. She was walking in circles, slow deliberate circles, with her head down, staring at her cupped hands like she was holding something. Her brow was furrowed. Her little lips were pressed together in concentration. She looked up, looked around at nobody, looked back down at her hands. Walked a few more steps. Stopped. Tapped her thumbs against the air.

My wife laughed first. That quick, involuntary laugh that comes out before you can stop it.

Then I saw it. She was being me. She was walking around the kitchen the way I walk around the house every single night. Head down. Phone in hand. Scrolling. Checking. Not seeing anyone. Not hearing anyone. Orbiting my own family like a satellite that's close enough to see the surface but never touches down.

I laughed. But it was the wrong kind of laugh. The kind that comes from a place closer to your stomach than your chest. The kind where your mouth is doing one thing and your insides are doing something else entirely.

Ayla saw it working. She jumped in. Started doing the same thing. Two little girls walking in circles, staring at imaginary phones, bumping into each other, giggling. My wife was cracking up. On the surface it was hilarious. Two kids doing a bit. Harmless.

But my wife's eyes told a different story. She was laughing, but I could see the thing underneath the laugh. The recognition. The quiet confirmation of something she'd been feeling for years but never said out loud because saying it would mean it was real. She knew. She'd always known. And now her daughters were performing it in the kitchen like a play she didn't buy tickets to.

I didn't say anything. I internalized everything. That's what I do. I stood there and let the moment wash over me, and I memorized every detail because I knew, even in real time, that I'd need to remember this later. That this was the kind of moment that changes how you see yourself if you're honest enough to let it.

My daughter didn't know what she'd done. She was six. She thought she was being funny. She was being funny. She was also holding up a mirror so clean and so close that I couldn't look away.

That night, after everyone was asleep, I sat at the table with my reMarkable. I like to write my goals by hand. There's something about the pen on the screen that makes it feel more binding than typing. Like you're signing a contract with yourself.

I wasn't writing new goals. I was reading old ones.

Three years of goals. Written at different tables in different houses at different stages of a life that moved so fast I barely recognized the handwriting from the earliest pages. Goals about revenue. About family. About the kind of man I wanted to become. Specific numbers. Specific milestones. Things I'd written at midnight, the same way I was sitting at midnight now, with the house dark and everyone I loved unconscious upstairs and nothing but the scratch of a stylus and the glow of a screen to keep me company.

I'd hit them. All of them. Every number. Every milestone. The revenue. The company. The family. The life. I was sitting inside the exact future I'd described to myself three years earlier. I'd arrived.

And the first thing I felt wasn't satisfaction. It was hunger.

What's next?

That question used to scare me. It used to feel like a curse. The inability to be content. The restlessness that made me build AYRA in a shower and eat cold meatballs in a dark kitchen and stare at a P&L at eighty miles per hour while my wife drove and my kids slept. The thing that made my daughter pick me out of a lineup at charades by walking in circles, staring at her hands.

But sitting there at that table, reading goals I'd already conquered, something settled over me. Not excitement. Not ambition. Something quieter than both. Like a warm blanket dropping over my shoulders on a night I didn't realize I was cold.

The goal was never the thing.

The goal was the version of myself I had to become to reach it. The fights I had to survive. The $2 million I had to lose and earn back. The employees who betrayed me and the ones who saved me. The wife who told me I'd be fine when I wasn't sure I would be. The father who told me it was okay when I needed someone to tell me it wasn't. The kitchen island with a sleeping baby and a $1,600 ad spend and a dream so fragile it could have shattered if one more thing went wrong.

The beauty was in the journey. It was always in the journey. Reaching the destination just shows you the next one.

The version of me in ten years will be different from the version sitting at this table. I hope he travels more. I hope he's more present. I hope his daughters never have to do that impression again because the man they're imitating finally learned to put the phone down.

But I know this about him: He won't be satisfied. He'll be chasing the next thing. And he'll be grateful for every mile between here and there because the miles are where the living happens.

A few weeks ago I was in Louisiana. Meeting with an attorney who'd just closed his third acquisition in two years. We finished dinner, and I was walking back to my car through a part of town I didn't know. I passed a storefront on a quiet block. The windows were dark. A faded awning. A sign for a nail salon or a copy shop, something that fills a space after the thing that mattered leaves. But underneath the new sign, where the stucco met the frame, there was a shadow. A rectangle slightly lighter than the wall around it, the kind of ghost a mounted sign leaves behind when someone pries it off and the sun hasn't finished erasing the outline.

I stopped. I don't know why. Something about the shape of that shadow. The size of it. Just right for a name and a title. The kind of sign a solo practitioner hangs the day the lease is signed, when the paint is fresh and the chairs are new and the phones haven't rung yet but you believe they will.

I stood there, and I could hear it. Not the street. The building. The version of it that used to exist. Phones ringing down a short hallway. A paralegal's voice asking a client to hold. A printer running. The particular hum of a small firm doing the work it was built to do, the sound of someone's life happening inside those walls, someone who went to law school and passed the bar and hung their name on the door because they wanted to help people.

I don't know if it was Jim's office. It probably wasn't. But I couldn't stop imagining that it was.

You picked up this book because something isn't working. Something about your firm, your life, or the gap between what you built and what you dreamed of building brought you to page one. You've stayed with me through Jim's porch and Sandy's wobbling chair and Maria's intake call and a hundred thousand dollars that turned into 5 signed cases and then 57. Through a $2 million loss and an AI built in a shower and a meatball dinner that went cold and a laptop locked inside an Escalade on a beach day in Margate.

I gave you everything I have. The system. The math. The psychology. The playbook. Every chapter was a piece of the machine, and the machine works. The proof is on the table. Tyler. Joey. Nick. A hundred and twenty firms and counting.

Now it's yours.

The window is open. The sharks are circling. And the only thing standing between the firm you have and the firm you could build is the decision to stop thinking about it and start.

Somewhere tonight, your daughter is walking in circles in the kitchen with her head down, staring at her cupped hands. She thinks it's funny. It is funny. It's also the most honest mirror you'll ever look into.

Put the phone down. Pick up the blueprint. Build something worth more than your fear.

And for God's sake, eat your meatballs while they're still warm.